Dave Pelz's
10 Minutes A Day to Better Putting

ALSO BY DAVE PELZ:

Dave Pelz's Short Game Bible

Dave Pelz's Putting Bible

Putt Like the Pros

<u>*Dave Pelz's*</u>

10 Minutes A Day to Better Putting

DAVE PELZ

with Eddie Pelz & James A. Frank

PELZ GOLF®

Published by The Pelz Golf Institute,

The Pelz Golf Institute
1310 Ranch Road 620 South
Suite B-1
Austin, TX 78734
800-833-7370 www.pelzgolf.com

Photo credits on page 189

ISBN: 1-58619-101-2
Library of Congress Catalog Number: 2003106276

Printed in the United States of America
April 2004
First Edition
07 06 05 04 2 3 4 5

Dedicated to Sherry

You are the best Sis ever. I hope you know that, and realize how much I appreciate your worrying about, advising, teaching, helping and protecting me as I've made my way.

You paved the way in the early years, making it possible for me to grow up happy, positive, carefree, and totally devoted to my basketball, and golf, always believing there were no problems you wouldn't handle. I wish all kids could have the good fortune of growing up with a big-Sis like you. I thank you for that.

Remember when you won all those matches playing "first-man" for our high school golf team, then got banned from the league because you were embarrassing the boys? I know how disappointed you were, yet never said a disparaging word. You've always been a class act, always a great example, and I love and respect you so much.

As a small token of my appreciation, I want to tell you in no uncertain terms that this book is for you. You've always objected to my telling so much of the why, when all you really wanted to know is how. Well, Sherry Beth, here it is, for you, how-to in pictures, with very few "*why*" distractions. I hope you improve your already incredibly good putting, and enjoy!

Love you! dp

Contents

Contents

Acknowledgements

We have a neat little company. We study and research the game of golf, we teach the scoring game (short game and putting) in 3-day schools (at 5 permanent locations) and 1-day clinics (in 42 cities), and we sell the equipment to both learn and play the scoring game better. Our team of 53 employees (33 in Austin, Texas) comprises the Pelz Golf Institute, customer service, graphics, information technology, finance, corporate services, human resources, product manufacturing, and shipping departments, plus 20 teaching professionals who live all over the country. We all work together to bring the best instruction, by the best instructors, at the finest facilities in the world, to you the golfer. This is the absolute goal of our efforts, and the purpose and devotion of our company.

I want to thank our team of 53 "team-family" members, for your caring and companionship. Life is a trip, and I'm glad we're on it together. I am so proud of the research, teaching, and services you provide in my name. Neither our teaching nor this book would be possible without you.

I also want to thank our good friends at our scoring game teaching facilities at the Boca Raton Resort and Club (Boca Raton, FL); Reynolds Plantation (Greensboro, GA); Cordillera Lodge and Spa (Edwards, CO); Homestead Resort (Traverse City, MI); Centennial Club (Carmel, NY) and Palm Springs, CA. Your staffs and beautiful facilities are wonderful to be involved with and we love being part of your team.

I want to especially recognize the efforts of our "book-team." In addition to my friends, the world's best golf photographer Leonard Kamsler and best golf editor Jim Frank, our internal bookers, under the able guidance of Joel Mendelman, are Bryan Allison, Adrian Reyes, Sven Nilson, David Watford and Eddie Pelz. You are all a pleasure to work with and your talents are awesome. Thank you all sincerely, and I hope your efforts will be reflected in the putting results of the golfers who use this book.

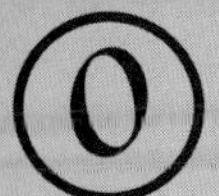

Introduction: Learning to Putt Better

What Can You Do in 10 Minutes?

By working on the right things, with the right attitude, and with the right use of feedback, you can improve your putting in just 10 minutes a day. In the following pages, I will show you how.

To putt better in any amount of time, you must do three things: you must learn *what* to improve, *how* to improve it, and then you must go *do* it.

Requirements for Better Putting

1) Learn ***WHAT*** needs to be improved

2) Learn ***HOW*** to improve it

3) ***DO IT*** (until it's committed to habit)

It has often been said that golf is a microcosm of life. Both depend on learning and preparation. Your success or failure in golf and in life is based largely on how well you prepare to succeed or fail. If you prepare to succeed in putting, you probably will, and this book can help you do just that. If you learn to prepare properly, then do it, you will putt better.

Learning happens in short periods of time. You could spend all day practicing, but your learning might occur in an instant. Or you might spend all day practicing and not learn a thing: Sometimes the light goes on, other times you remain in the dark.

Of course, you can't achieve all your goals–say, becoming the world's best putter–in just 10 minutes. But have no doubt: By working on your putting in a series of positive, intelligent, focused, 10-Minute Learning Sessions with good feedback, you can learn enough to achieve your putting goals. That's a promise.

Is This Book for You?

"10 Minutes a Day to Better Putting" is a "how-to" book. It is a collection of photographs, captions, and short bits of instruction designed to show you how to improve and groove various aspects of putting in 10-Minute Sessions.

"10 Minutes" doesn't have much to say about "why" things should be done (if you want to know why, read my "Putting Bible"). 10 minutes won't help golfers who merely *wish, hope, dream,* or *want* to putt better. This is my "*don't-ask-me-why, just shut-up-and-do-it*" book. Hey, if nothing else, I'm being honest.

This book also encourages you to buy and use learning aids. They don't have to be the learning aids shown in these pages (these are just the ones developed by the Pelz Golf Institute, for use in our schools and clinics). There are other good learning aids too, and I encourage you to evaluate and use them if they provide the necessary feedback. What you must realize is that if you want to improve your putting, you *must* use learning aids. Because no matter how hard you work, you can't improve without feedback.

That's right. *If you don't receive immediate, accurate, and reliable feedback on what you're doing, right or wrong, as you work on your putting, you are wasting your time. In fact, you may be hurting your putting more than helping it.* So, unless you are willing to devote 10 minute capsules of time to improve your putting, and use learning aids, this book is not for you.

The Goal of This Book

It's very simple. I want to show anyone willing to devote 10 minutes at a time, how to improve his (or her) putting. Suggestions for doing so are presented on yellow pad notes marked with a 10 minute clock icon throughout the book. If you want to work longer, combine these sessions. Want to work for an hour? Try six 10-Minute Sessions. Have half an hour a day to devote to putting? Then try three 10-Minute Sessions. But if you can't make at least one 10 minute block of time available at least several days a week, you'll just have to be content with what you are doing now, and the results it brings you.

I've Seen It Happen

Think 10 minutes a day isn't enough? Done right, it is. I've seen the lights go on in a golfer's mind (or muscles) in 10 minutes and his putting improve dramatically—and permanently. It may take hours, days, even weeks of preparation (learning sessions) before you are ready to learn and internalize something that really will help your putting. But then, in one 10-Minute Session, you "get it." And once internalized, it's yours forever.

When your putting habits improve, you putt better out of habit. Improving your putting is like walking a mile: Each step is easy, but it takes a lot of them to get there. Similarly, you can improve your putting one 10-Minute Session at a time, but it may take a lot of them to make a real difference.

If you have one good 10-Minute Session a day, it may take you several years (up to five if you're a true beginner) to putt your best. But try more than one session some days, and work on grooving more than one skill at a time (as you'll see in Chapter 7), then success will come much faster. One session a day is like walking. But once you get into shape and can start running, you get there a lot faster.

Why Not Just "Feel" It?

What about those golfers who don't improve with practice? Or those who actually get worse? After such negative experiences, they think practice must make them too technical or mechanical. They tell themselves (and others) that they must be "feel" players. "Forget all that practice," they say. "It doesn't help. Just putt with feel".

However, 28 years of research and teaching has proven to me, that few golfers putt well by clearing their minds and just "feeling" putts. Most golfers putt poorly because, clear minds or not, they have poor putting strokes, poor touch, poor feel, or don't know how to read greens.

Another old wives' tale is that good putting requires practice, practice, and more practice. That's wrong, too. Millions of golfers practice their hearts out; only to putt worse than when they started. If you don't know what to practice or how to practice it, no amount of practice will help you get better. Practice does not make perfect. Practice makes permanent.

If you practice poorly, you will become a permanently poor putter. And I say you deserve it.

To improve your putting, you need to work on the right things, in the right way. That's what 10-Minute Sessions are for.

The Road to Improvement

These are the essential skills of putting. Like a real pyramid, the base is wide, strong, and stable, while the top is small and focused. Which aspects of your putting need improvement? Do you know?

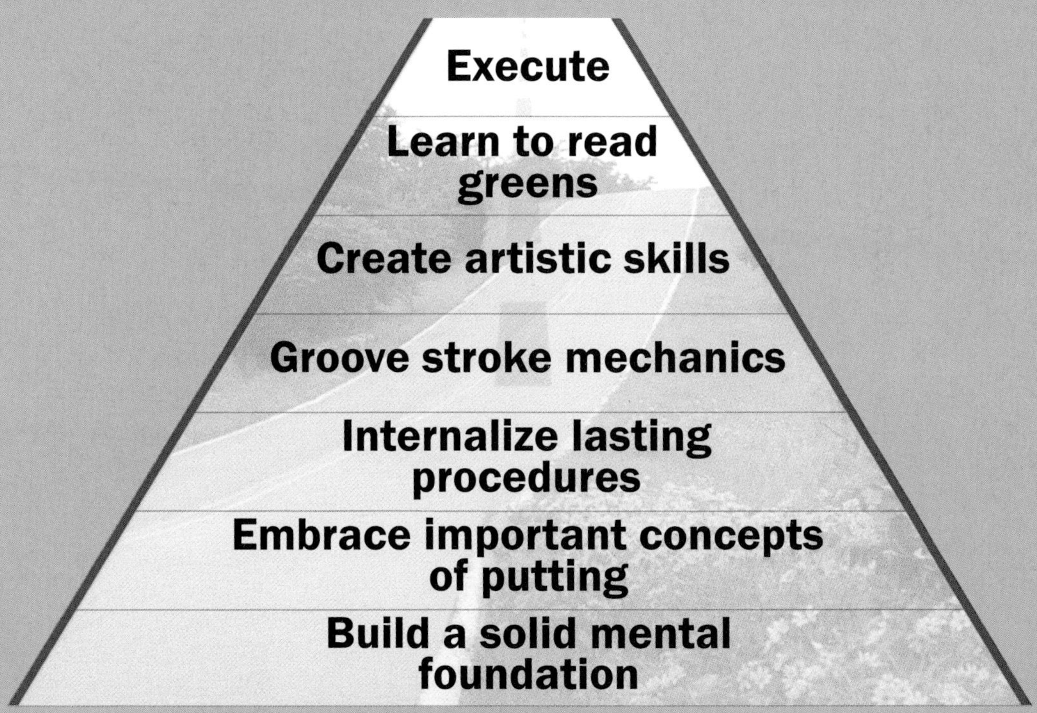

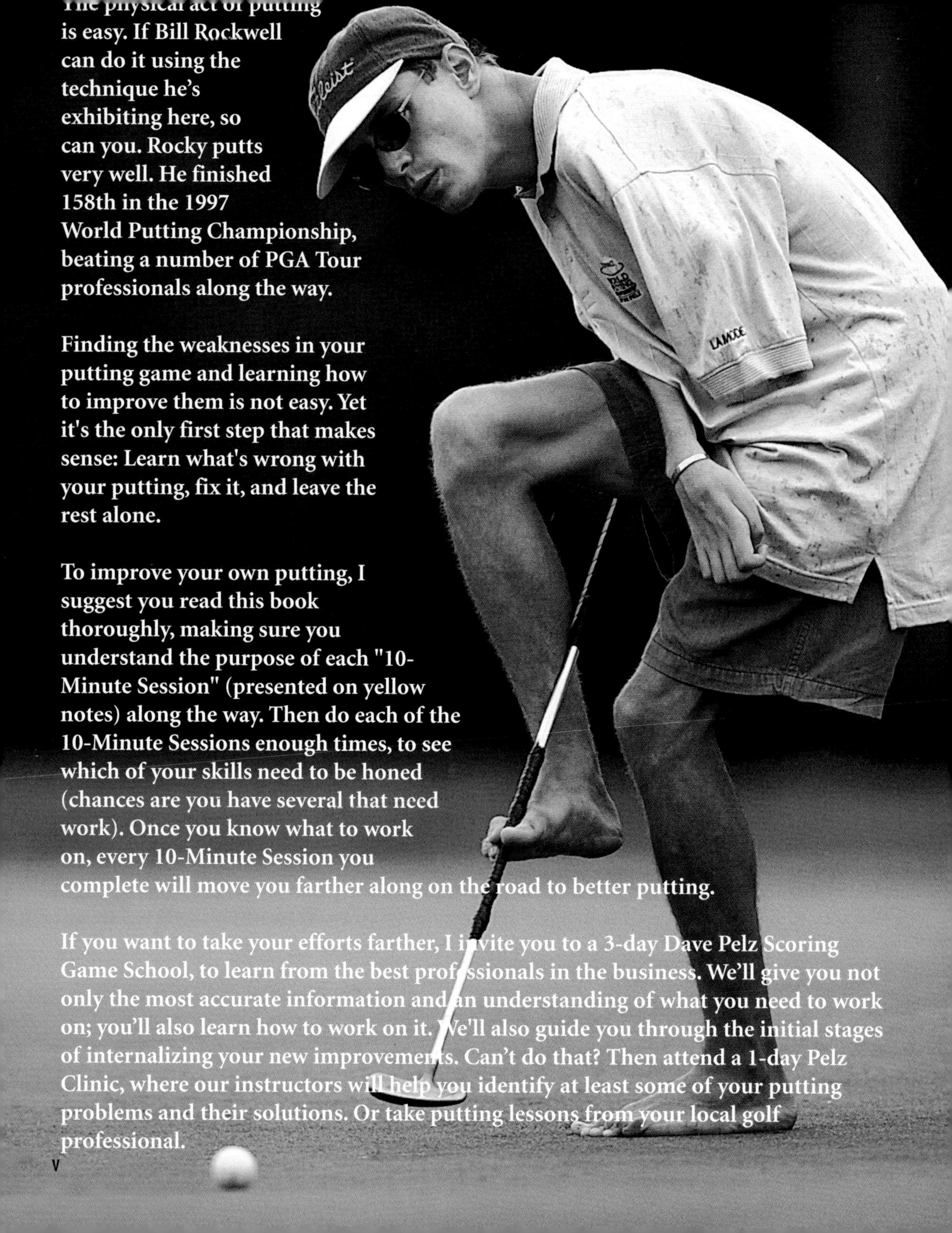

The physical act of putting is easy. If Bill Rockwell can do it using the technique he's exhibiting here, so can you. Rocky putts very well. He finished 158th in the 1997 World Putting Championship, beating a number of PGA Tour professionals along the way.

Finding the weaknesses in your putting game and learning how to improve them is not easy. Yet it's the only first step that makes sense: Learn what's wrong with your putting, fix it, and leave the rest alone.

To improve your own putting, I suggest you read this book thoroughly, making sure you understand the purpose of each "10-Minute Session" (presented on yellow notes) along the way. Then do each of the 10-Minute Sessions enough times, to see which of your skills need to be honed (chances are you have several that need work). Once you know what to work on, every 10-Minute Session you complete will move you farther along on the road to better putting.

If you want to take your efforts farther, I invite you to a 3-day Dave Pelz Scoring Game School, to learn from the best professionals in the business. We'll give you not only the most accurate information and an understanding of what you need to work on; you'll also learn how to work on it. We'll also guide you through the initial stages of internalizing your new improvements. Can't do that? Then attend a 1-day Pelz Clinic, where our instructors will help you identify at least some of your putting problems and their solutions. Or take putting lessons from your local golf professional.

Yes You Can!

Don't let anyone tell you that you can't putt better. Every golfer has putting weaknesses, which means you can improve whether you are a student at one of our schools (amateurs drop roughly 4 strokes a round in the first year after attending a school), or one of the best players in the world.

I've watched many golfers improve their putting, including two of the very best, Phil Mickelson and Vijay Singh. Phil improved from 80th to second in the PGA Tour putting stats, while Vijay moved from 139th to fourth. They were good putters before I worked with them, and you might have thought they didn't have much to improve. But they have improved, by doing exactly what you're about to do: identifying their weaknesses and improving them, one session at a time.

If they can do it, why can't you?

① Build a Sound Foundation

The mind perceives a putt. The body executes a stroke. The ball rolls. That's putting.

The perception must come first because your mind controls your body, your body controls your putter, and your putter instructs the ball in what direction and how fast to roll. A healthy mind loaded with sharp images and concise vision can move a putter with clarity and confidence. A well-trained mind working together with the body and with accurate understanding of the conditions, can achieve amazing things. However, if the mind falters, hesitates, or is confused, even a well-grooved stroke can produce disastrous results on the greens.

It all starts in your mind. That's where you house your vision of how good putting is performed, your mental attitude toward putting, your philosophy of learning from feedback, and your beliefs concerning your own putting stroke. Combined, they form the foundation of your putting. So, first things first. Before you start worrying about stroke mechanics, be sure your head is screwed on straight.

Improve Your Attitude

A positive, determined, patient, disciplined attitude is necessary for good putting. Saying or knowing this however, does not give you a great attitude.

You can't simply tell yourself to be positive and have a good attitude and have it be so, unless you are blessed with good-attitude genes (which some people are). Unfortunately, most golfers have to deal with negative vibrations, which they can find almost anywhere they look. Insecurity, doubt, pessimism, anxiety, fear of the unknown, and negative past experiences make it hard to develop good attitudes. This is why so many golfers (and especially those with bad-attitude genes) have little to no chance of ever reaching their full potential. But attitudes, like putting strokes, can be improved. The key is the right sort of work.

Read and Learn

If you have a great attitude, skip to the next section. However, if you're not totally convinced that you can become a great putter, it's time to begin learning the realities of putting. Knowledge is a powerful tool for building understanding and confidence. I explain the facts of putting in my "Putting Bible"; reading it will help ground your expectations in reality and provide some useful encouragement.

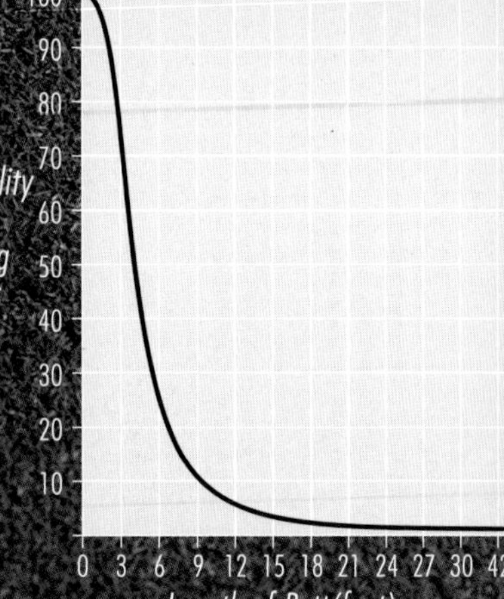

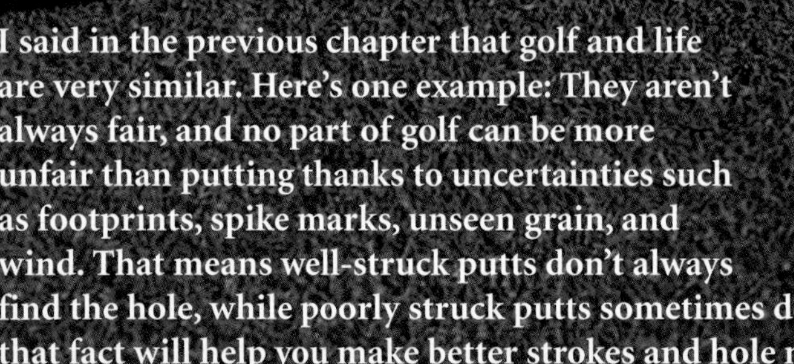

I said in the previous chapter that golf and life are very similar. Here's one example: They aren't always fair, and no part of golf can be more unfair than putting thanks to uncertainties such as footprints, spike marks, unseen grain, and wind. That means well-struck putts don't always find the hole, while poorly struck putts sometimes do. Accepting that fact will help you make better strokes and hole more putts.

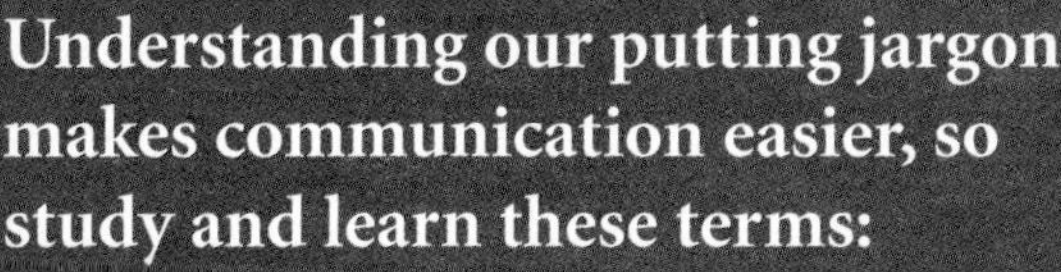

Understanding our putting jargon makes communication easier, so study and learn these terms:

Aimline: Line (direction) on which you intend to aim your putter, body, stroke, and start your putt rolling

Ball-hole line: Straight line between ball and cup

Visible break: Maximum distance ball track separates from ball-hole line

True break point: Point on Aimline at same distance from ball as hole

Ball Track: Path along which the ball rolls

True break Distance from near edge of hole to true break point

Good mental health is essential for optimum performance. "Golf is Not a Game of Perfect," by sports psychologist Bob Rotella, is a great read. While not just about putting, it provides an understanding of how well you can play, and why you can practice and play for enjoyment as well as for score.

"The Inner Game of Golf," by W. Timothy Gallwey, one of the first psychology books written on golf, can help you better understand how your mind affects your performance both on and off the course. That knowledge will help you come to terms with the patience, self-control, self-discipline, rigors of learning and change required for improvement.

Attitude and Goals

Organize and write down your goals. I don't mean your goal to putt better and shoot lower scores, but for working on your game and preparing an attitude that will lead to success. The following are examples of what I personally have decided (once you see yours in writing, they become more real, and more realizable).

My Attitude Will Be:

1) Positive: I *believe* I can develop into a good putter, learn to consistently lag putts dead to the hole, and make more than my share of putts.
2) Determined: I will *commit* to improving my putting. I will *do the drills*, 10minutes at a time, required to achieve improvement.
3) Stubborn: I will *refuse* to get discouraged for more than a few minutes at a time, ever again.
4) Patient:I know I won't become a great putter overnight. It will take time, repetition, careful and effective work, and above all, *patience*. I know my body will occasionally make terrible strokes, for no apparent reason other than to test my resolve and patience. I will deal with it.
5) Optimistic: I will *focus* on small signs of improvement as I pursue a better putting game.
6) Can Do: There is no putt I cannot make. No matter how difficult, I will *make a good stroke*. Who knows? I may get lucky.

Will you ever reach your goals? Probably, if they are realistic. Will you ever get as good as a Tour professional? Maybe. In putting, unlike almost every other part of the game, it is very possible. How good can you get? This is your opportunity to find out.

My Goals

1) Lower my handicap to +2.
2) Consistently beat Clayton and TJ, as they age.
3) Shoot better than my age 15 times.
4) Complete a round in which I stroked every putt absolutely as well as I possibly could.
5) Beat Phil and Vijay in a short game session.

#1 Learn *what* before you work on *how*: Read Rotella and Gallwey until you finish both books, then spend a 10-Minute Session writing down your goals. Understand that your mind doesn't hit the golf ball. Your mind cannot move the ball into the hole by willpower alone. But your mind controls your body, which controls your putter, which controls your instructions to your putts. Remember, it all starts in your mind. That's why goals and attitude are important.

Create a Vision

Most golfers can't describe what good putting is, how a good putting stroke moves, or what one feels and looks like. Asked to do so, they usually respond, "A good putter makes the ball go in the hole." Then they laugh, as if their answer is really a joke. I like a good joke as much as the next person, but not knowing what it is you are trying to do, or how you should look doing it, isn't funny. It is a serious detriment to success.

There are two kinds of golfers who want to putt better: Those who wish or hope it will happen, and those who are determined to make it happen. If you are satisfied with wishing and hoping your putts will start falling, then put down this book.

If, however, you are willing to work to improve your putting, you need a vision of what you're trying to do and how you should look doing it. You need a vision to focus on, work toward, and judge your progress against.

See How You Should Look

Watch all the great putters you can, and file away (for later recall) the vision of what you are trying to do in your "mind's eye." As you work on your putting, your brain will begin to recognize what it's looking for in a great stroke. The more good images of good strokes you've filed away, the easier it becomes to learn to make them yourself.

Phil Mickelson has a great conventional stroke

Vijay Singh uses the body putter best

Bruce Lietzke is the model for long putting

See How You Do Look

Small, powerful video-camcorders are great for creating "almost real-time" feedback as you learn to putt better. If you have one, use it. If you don't have one, get one.

10 minute

#2 Create and refine a vision: To watch the best in person, attend PGA and LPGA Tour events early in the week, before the tournament starts, when the pros are working on their putting. (That's right: Good as they are, they are always working on their strokes.) Spend 10 minutes watching the leading money-winners on the practice green. Try to watch standing face-on and down-target (from behind), following their stroke motions from both angles. Focus on the movement of the putter head, and how their arms and putter shaft swing. Concentrate on their rhythmic motions and imagine them coming from your body. Back at home, watch the video of your strokes and look for differences. Over time, those differences will go away.

Adopt a Learning Philosophy

There's a lot to learn in golf: rules, ball-flight laws, how shots react, the fundamentals of swing mechanics, and so on. There's more than one way to learn, as well. There's intellectual understanding, the feel of physical moves, muscle memories, touch for good putting, and so on. In both cases, there is so much, that nobody ever gets it all.

Fortunately, our brains can handle all we cram into them. So, the real problem with learning to putt better is trying to see, become aware of, and internalize enough good information to make a difference in the amount of time you are willing to spend on it.

To make the most of your time (to optimize your exposure to good information while eliminating bad) follow these three rules: 1) Never practice without accurate feedback on what you're doing right or wrong; 2) Create a convenient place where you can work with the necessary equipment for 10-Minute Learning Sessions; and 3) Train to absolute values that never change. Here's what I mean by each one.

Commit to Feedback

The Key To Efficient 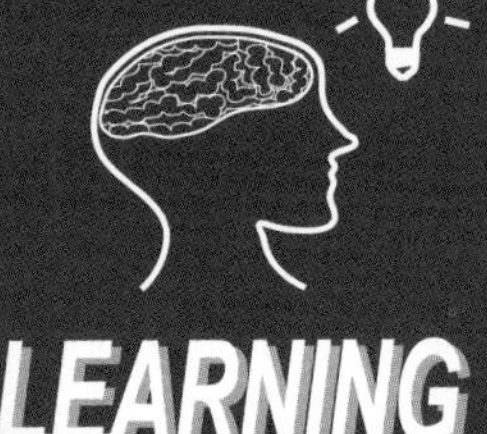

= Immediate Accurate Reliable 

Make a bad driver swing on the range and you see a bad drive. Make a bad 9-iron swing, hit behind the ball, and you see a fat shot. When practicing the full swing, your shots show what you did, right or wrong, and based on this feedback, you make improvements.

Putting is different. Balls are rolling on an unknown surface, and encountering conditions no one can see or predict (footprints, spike marks, wind, unknown speed and break). Well-stroked putts often miss the hole, while poorly stroked ones sometimes go in. The results don't always match the efforts, so golfers don't know if what they did was good or bad. A good stroke can still produce a miss because the break was miss-read. So they change their stroke, make the next putt, and think they improved, when, in reality, a spike mark knocked the ball in. And then they wonder why they don't putt better on the course.

Working on putting without accurate feedback is a waste of time. Commit to always practicing with a learning aid. This is the only way to know the truth about your performance. The hole is not a learning aid.

Create Access to Feedback

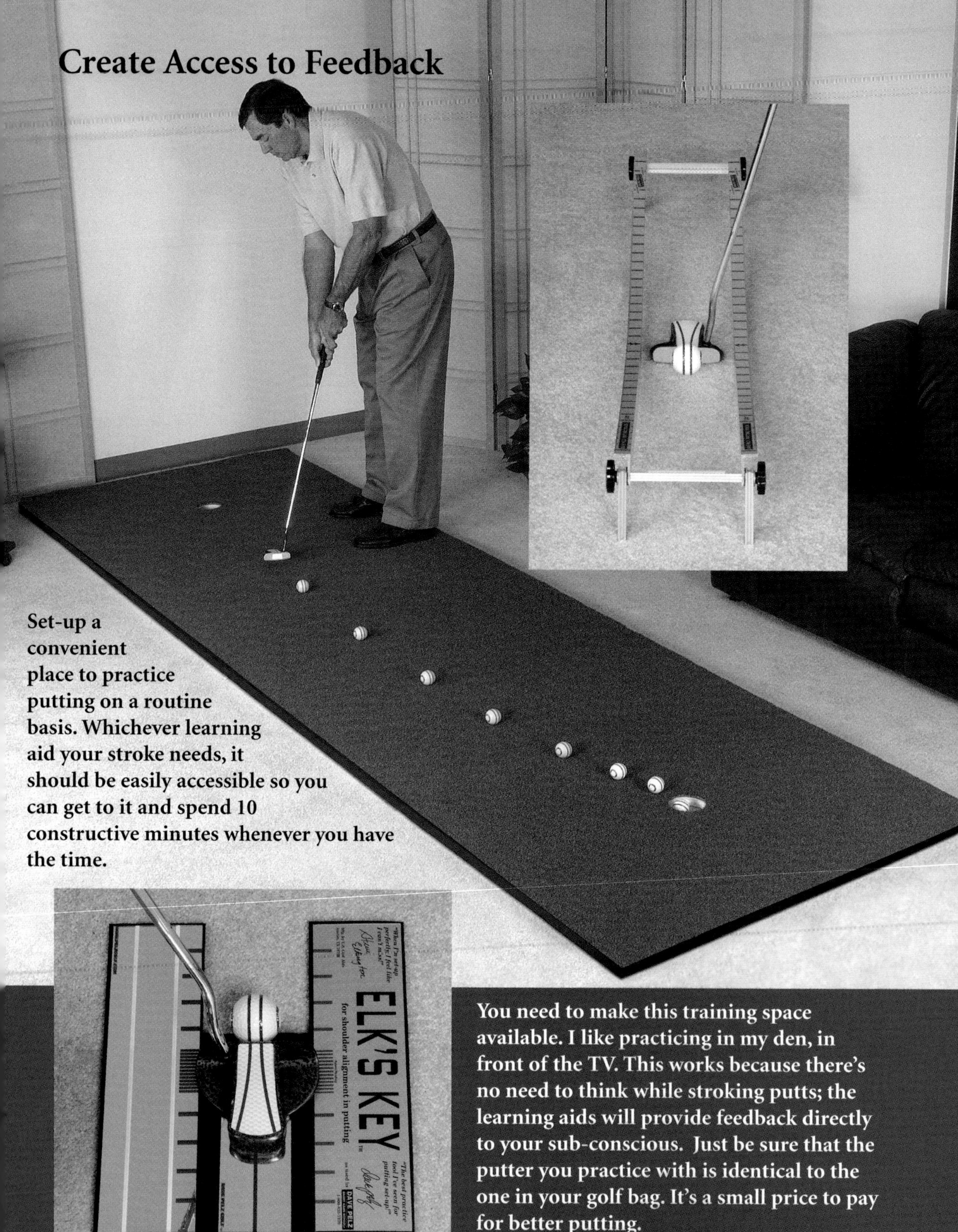

Set-up a convenient place to practice putting on a routine basis. Whichever learning aid your stroke needs, it should be easily accessible so you can get to it and spend 10 constructive minutes whenever you have the time.

You need to make this training space available. I like practicing in my den, in front of the TV. This works because there's no need to think while stroking putts; the learning aids will provide feedback directly to your sub-conscious. Just be sure that the putter you practice with is identical to the one in your golf bag. It's a small price to pay for better putting.

Train to Absolutes

How do most golfers practice putting? They step on the putting green, drop a few balls, try a new stance or grip (like their friend used the other day), take a few raps, and think that if the ball goes into the hole, they're doing something good.

There is a better way, and the recipe is simple: Make sure it's right, keep it simple, keep it constant, and rehearse it over and over again with accurate feedback. Soon it will become a habit.

The key phrase there is "make sure it's right." How do you do that? That's what this book and all the feedback devices you see in it, are all about.

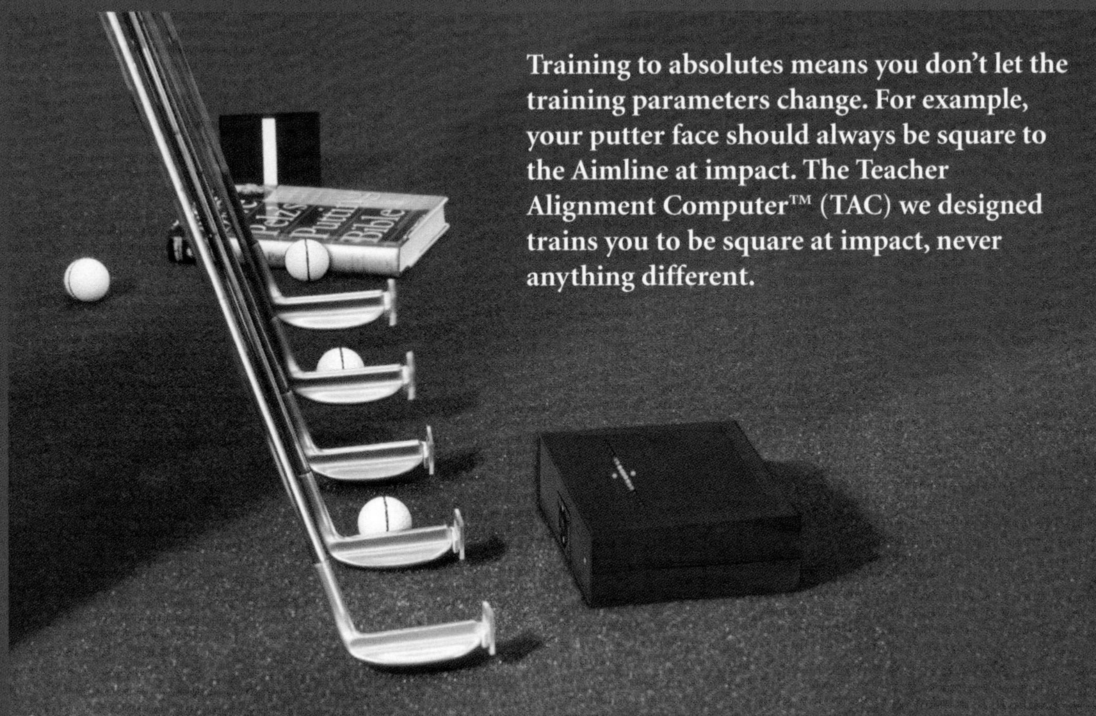

Training to absolutes means you don't let the training parameters change. For example, your putter face should always be square to the Aimline at impact. The Teacher Alignment Computer™ (TAC) we designed trains you to be square at impact, never anything different.

#3 Commit to feedback: After you've finished reading this book, when you decide which aspects of your stroke need improvement, you will acquire some learning aids. Before haphazardly dropping them somewhere, choose one place that you can devote to most of your 10-Minute Sessions. Clear that space, set up your learning aids, and make sure your spouse, kids, pets, and guests understand that this area, and the learning aids in it, are not to be disturbed. This is important, as you don't want to spend time re-setting the equipment. After that, it's just repetition.

Relate Practice to Play

Why practice putting? So you are prepared to putt better on the course.
Playing is about the enjoyment of the outdoors, camaraderie, and competition (with others or the course itself). Enjoyment also comes with playing better, and for many golfers, that can come with better putting.

I mention all this because most golfers don't practice the same way they putt on the course, and they don't putt on the course the same way they practiced. It's no wonder they don't putt better after practicing.

Because you are reading this book, you have made a commitment to spend the time and energy necessary to improve your putting. To make the most of that time, follow these rules:

1) Spend about equal time practicing and playing. This will optimize your scoring, assuming you practice well and it carries over to your play.
2) Distribute your practice time equally among full swing, short game, and putting (1/3 to each).
3) Always practice putting the same way you intend to putt on the course.
4) Always putt on the course exactly as you practiced.

Understand Practice

Putting obeys the "weakest-link" law. The worst aspect of your putting is the one that will break the chain. Most golfers practice their strengths and avoid their weaknesses because it's more fun. Don't follow that example. Identify and work on your problems (for example, if holing short putts is a problem, practice the short-putt drills).

Practice ≠ Perfect

Practice = Permanent

I'd like to get my hands on the person who first told golfers "practice makes perfect." It isn't true, and has messed up more golf games than you can imagine. But millions of golfers believe the three ingredients of putting success are practice, practice, and more practice. They are wrong, wrong, and more wrong.

Practice doesn't make perfect. Practice makes permanent.

Practice Like You Play, Play Like You Practice

The best way to putt under pressure is to have grooved a routine and ritual that you execute before every putt in practice, then stay faithful to it. You want to stroke important putts just the way you stroked practice putts thousands of times on the practice green.

#4 Plan for just two weeks: Sit down with a pencil and a pad of paper. Think through how often, on which days, and at what times you will work on your putting. (This does not mean the few minutes of stroking some practice putts before heading out to play your weekend round.) Map out a two-week schedule of 10-Minute Learning Sessions, commit to it, then do it. I'll bet that by the time you sit down to map out the following two weeks, you'll begin to see the effects of the first two weeks. Congratulations: You're on your way.

2 Concepts of Good Putting

Having developed a good mental foundation from Chapter 1, the next step is to identify the challenges to your success. The goal is to become aware of the difference between the old wives' tales, pitfalls, and stumbling blocks most golfers succumb to and the fundamentals on which you can hang your hat.

If you don't understand cause and effect in putting, you can't diagnose what's going wrong in a round and deal with it. If you don't develop a stable stroke through impact, if your putts don't roll at or near optimum speed, or you don't understand that random error plays a significant role on the greens, you'll never putt anywhere near

your potential. If your putter, set-up, and grip won't allow you to make good strokes, you can't spend enough time practicing to overcome them. If your putting posture makes your back hurt, you won't spend significant time putting, and you'll never enjoy the game as you should.

However, don't let the negatives put you off. Even though there are many ways to miss putts and many excuses for bad putting, none of them need be inherent in your game. By understanding a few underlying but important concepts, you can avoid the problems most golfers never solve and build a putting game guaranteed to be statistically successful.

Recognize Unseen Factors

Just because something isn't obvious doesn't mean it's not important. For example, it's hard to see the difference between when golfers accelerate or decelerate their putters into impact. Yet, it makes a very big difference. Accelerating putters have stability, which minimizes twist, wobble, energy loss, and direction change when they don't strike putts on the sweet-spot. (And yes, you will miss your putter's sweet-spot on occasion. Every human does.)

Another subtle aspect of putting is knowing whether or not putts are rolling at their optimum speed. Everybody knows that if you roll balls too fast, they won't stay in the hole; too slow and they don't get to it. But what speed is optimum? And what about imparting "hook-overspin" spin on putts, as rumor has it that Ben Crenshaw does? Do his putts really roll with overspin and dive into the cup? Is that what makes him a great putter? And what's this about random luck and statistics? Read on!

Stability is Crucial

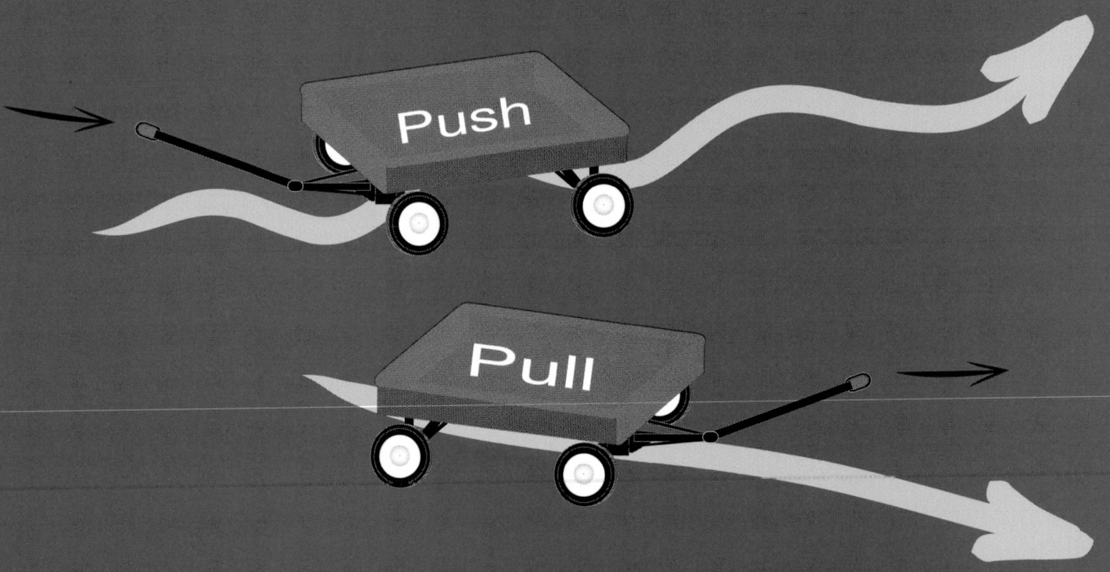

Little red wagons are stable when pulled, unstable when pushed. It is a law of physics that when a force pulls a mass, the mass must follow the force. When the same force pushes the mass however, it can move or turn in many directions depending on where the force pushes relative to the center of the mass. The same law applies to putters and golf balls.

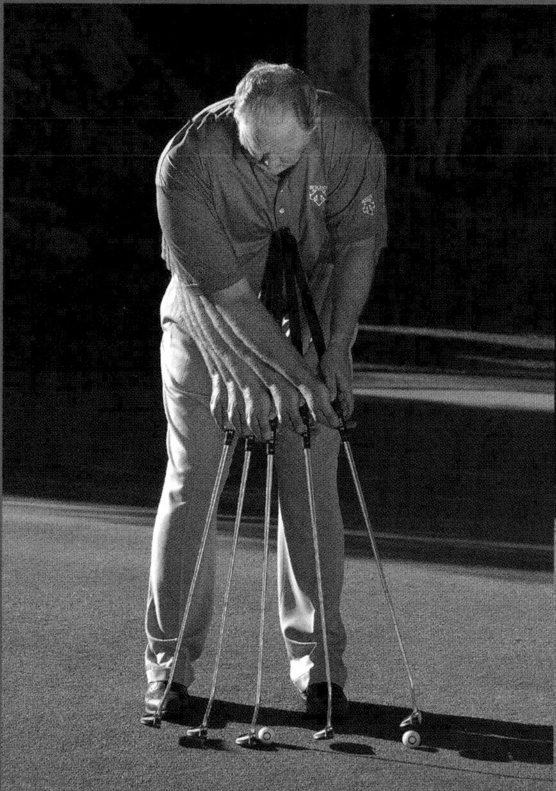

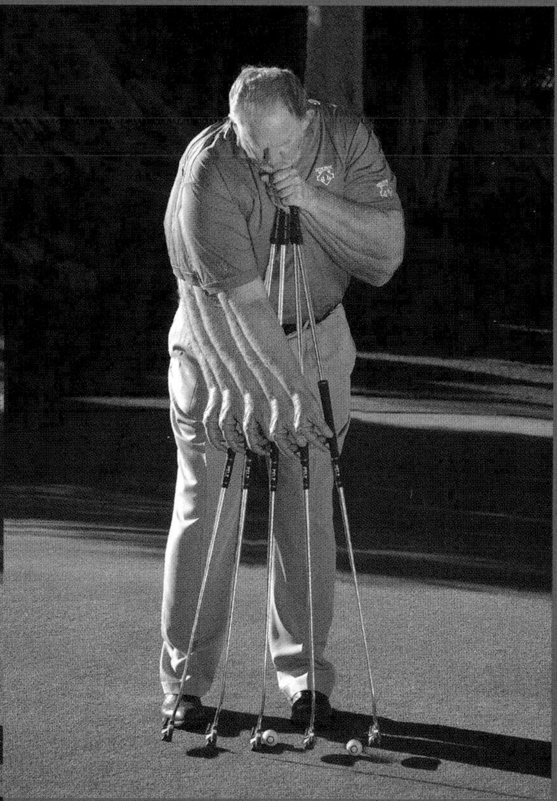

The putter's stability is largely dependent on whether it is accelerating (speeding up) or decelerating (slowing down) at the moment of impact. A pulled, accelerating stroke is more stable, and reduces head rotation, twisting, and energy loss more than a decelerating (slowing) stroke on miss-hits.

This does not mean you should "muscle" your putter to accelerate it through putts. A better way to produce a stable, gently accelerating stroke is to make the length of your follow-through slightly longer than the length of your back swing. This applies to all length putters.

Optimum Speed : 17 inches past (and the lumpy donut)

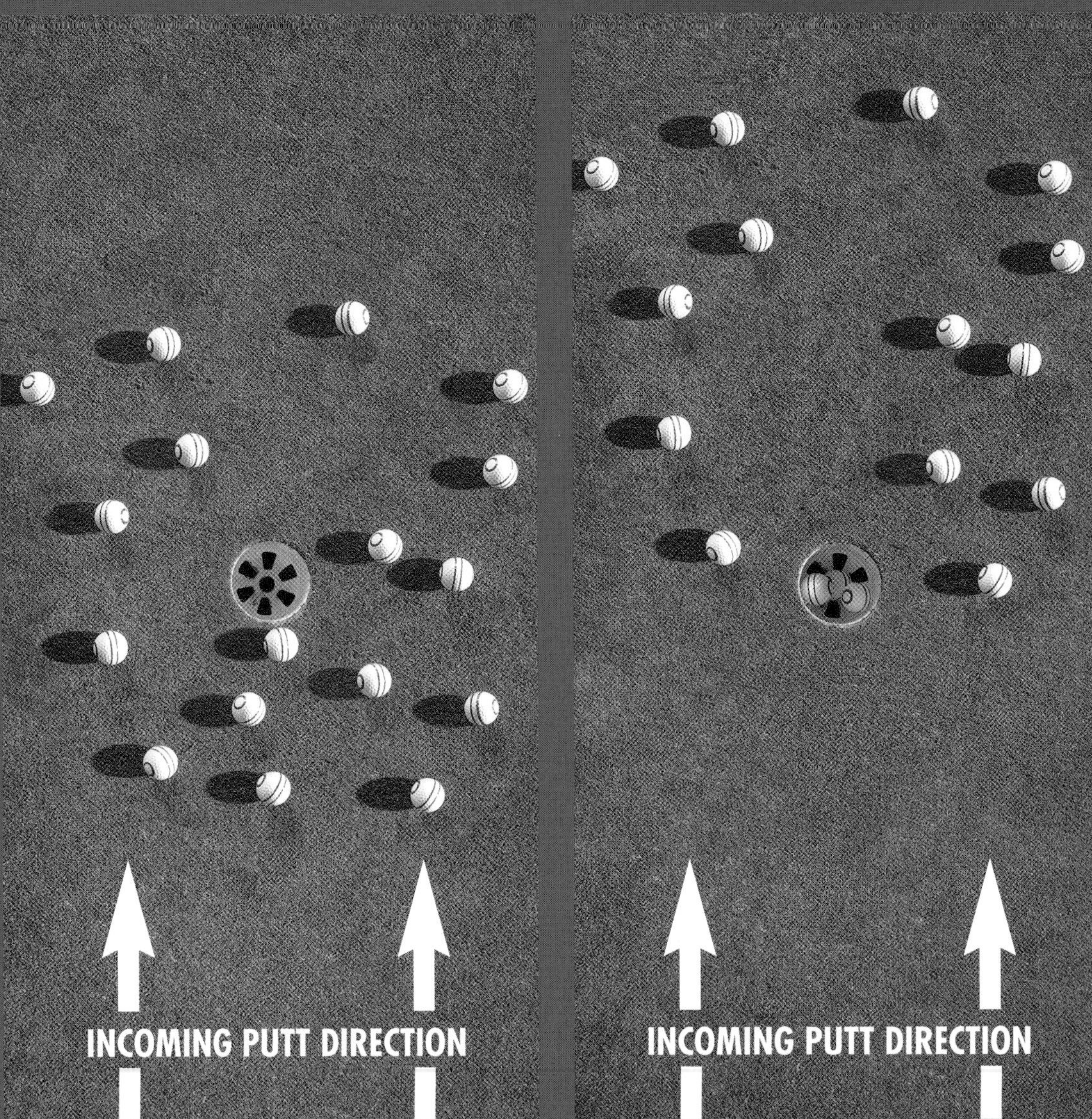

Putts that don't have enough speed to reach the hole have no chance of going in. Golfers leaving half of their putts short give up half of their chances of "getting lucky".

Look what happens when all putts have enough speed to roll past the hole (in same dispersion pattern as on left). Getting to the hole means all putts have a chance to get lucky and fall in. A "17-inches-past" speed also lets them hold their line better through the lumpy-donut (the area around the hole where virtually all golfers walk), so more hit the hole without rolling so fast as to lip-out.

Backspin, Sidespin, Overspin, Whatspin

Question: Do you want overspin, topspin, backspin, sidespin, or hook spin on putts?
Answer: None of the above.

If balls nearing the hole were spinning like the Roadrunner's feet or the wheels of a drag racer, your putting would suffer severely. Once the spinning ball "caught" or "grabbed" the green surface, it would jump quickly forward, backward, or straight sideways, depending on the direction of the spin.

Grass friction removes spin from putts early in their roll, so putts are never spinning as they roll slowly near the cup. Initial backspin or overspin caused by striking balls above or below center, both cause inconsistent roll, so you don't want either of these. The ideal putt starts sliding, then rolling on top of the grass, not down into, through, or bouncing on it.

Initial sidespin, which can be imparted by an open or closed putter face, or bad putter path at impact, causes off-line starts. Again, no spin is the best spin.

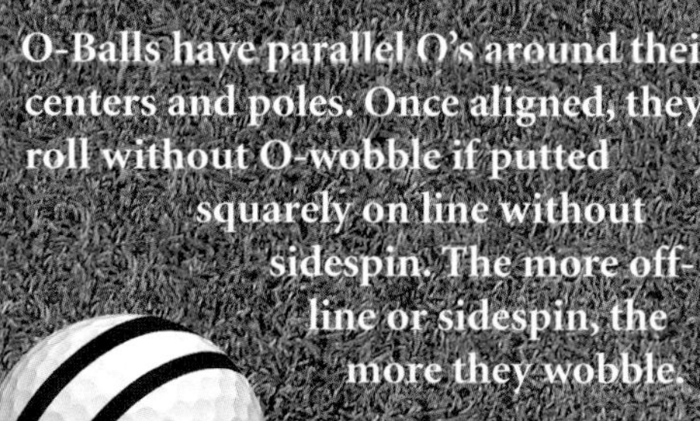

O-Balls have parallel O's around their centers and poles. Once aligned, they roll without O-wobble if putted squarely on line without sidespin. The more off-line or sidespin, the more they wobble.

A pure O-Ball roll (zero wobble) means it rolled precisely on its Aimline, so where it ends up shows if the golfer's aim was correct for the slope of the green, or not.

Because of their feedback principles, O-Balls are used in our schools and throughout this book.

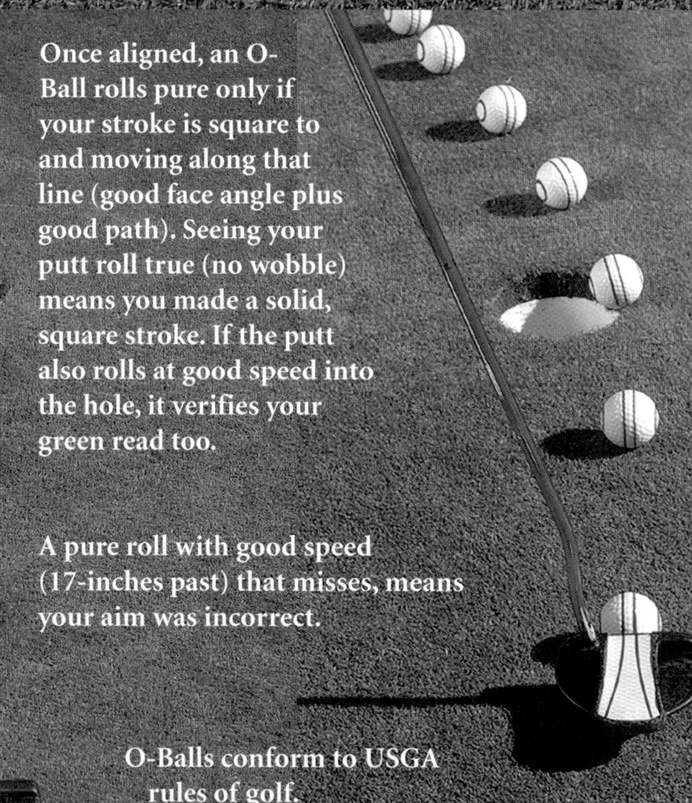

Once aligned, an O-Ball rolls pure only if your stroke is square to and moving along that line (good face angle plus good path). Seeing your putt roll true (no wobble) means you made a solid, square stroke. If the putt also rolls at good speed into the hole, it verifies your green read too.

A pure roll with good speed (17-inches past) that misses, means your aim was incorrect.

O-Balls conform to USGA rules of golf.

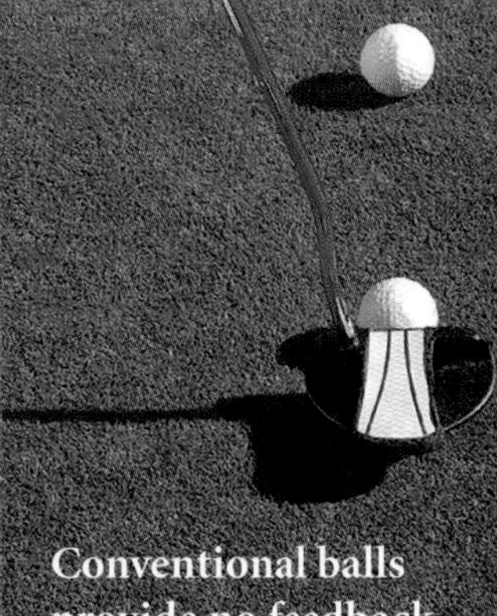

Conventional balls provide no feedback on your putting or green-reading, good or bad.

Cut-strokes cannot roll O-Balls without wobble.

When an O-Ball wobbles and misses, no green read information is available from a poorly stroked putt.

Putting O-Balls is an advantage (in practice and on course): learn if your putts start on-line or not; were they hit with side spin or not; was the amount of break played accurate or not.

#5 Learn from every putt: Spend 10 minutes on a practice green putting one O-Ball, always properly aligned, to random holes. Watch each putt roll and ask yourself:
1) Was my follow through longer than my back stroke?
2) Did my O-Ball show wobble (how square was my stroke)?
3) How far past the cup did the ball roll (too much or too little speed)?
4) Did I read the right break (based on #2 and #3 above)?

The goal is to form a habit: watch and learn from every putt, in practice or on the course. The quicker you learn the difference between good and bad strokes, the better you will putt.

Stroke Characteristics and Influences

Look at the sports images on these two pages and understand: each motion can be executed down the line without rotation, or around the body with lots of rotation. The same is true for putting.

Most golfers have been told the putter should rotate around the body in the putting stroke. In truth, your putter should or should not rotate depending on how you hold it and how you stand. Also, the more a putter rotates, the less time it spends square to the line and the harder it is to start a ball on the Aimline. Furthermore, golfers instinctively putt with their hands (since they do so many other things in life with their hands), but the more they rely on hand power (and wrist motion) the more variability enters into their strokes and the worse they putt.

The length of your putter, your posture, and your putting technique all effect how your putter swings. Because of the differences in golfers' bodies and equipment, there is no one perfect putting motion for all golfers. But there is one perfect motion for you, with your putter. Learn how your putter should swing before you try to groove it.

Pure-In-Line-Square (PILS) vs. Screen Door Motions

Rotation around the spine produces power; swinging down the line produces accuracy. The ability to move objects in accurate directions is important in many sports, and rotation is not good for this purpose. Therefore, when it comes to putting, less rotation is better.

When my putting robot Perfy's® (or any other golfer's) hands hang vertically below his shoulders, his putter path is pure-in-line and square (PILS) with the Aimline. No putter face rotation, no open or closed face angles, no inside or outside stroke motion. Timing and ball position are relatively unimportant to this stroke.

When a putter swings around a golfer's spine, the result is significant face rotation. A rotating face is only square to the Aimline for an instant, giving the golfer zero margin for error in timing. Timing and ball position are critical to this stroke. But timing a rotating putter is like trying to be somewhere exactly on time: you're usually a little early or a little late! In putting, that means starting the ball either right or left of the Aimline.

Style Determines Rotation

A conventional-length putter can swing pure-in-line or around the body, depending on how the hands swing under (left) or around the suspension point (right).

The long putter swings with almost no face rotation when it is suspended almost vertically under the chin.

The higher the anchor point and closer to vertical a body putter swings, the less it will rotate. Try various anchor points before choosing one.

Wrist Hinge and Body Motion

Ben Hogan's poor putting drove him prematurely from the game.

In Ben Hogan's day, greens were very slow. He needed lots of power, which he got by hinging his wrists during the stroke. Hogan's way should not be yours. The less you use your hands and wrists, the better your putting.

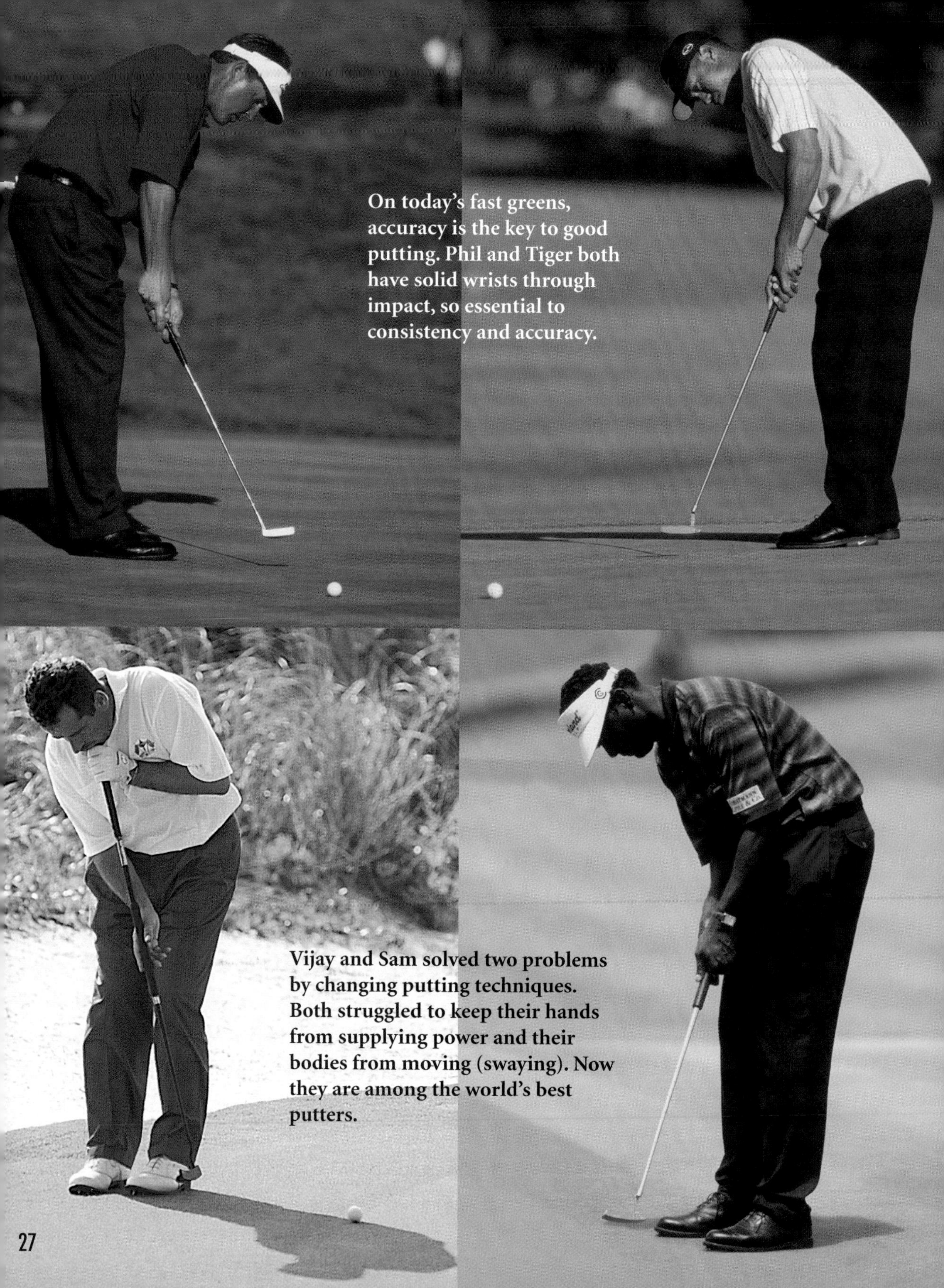

On today's fast greens, accuracy is the key to good putting. Phil and Tiger both have solid wrists through impact, so essential to consistency and accuracy.

Vijay and Sam solved two problems by changing putting techniques. Both struggled to keep their hands from supplying power and their bodies from moving (swaying). Now they are among the world's best putters.

With the exception of putting, every shot in golf depends on forearm rotation for power. When starting the game, golfers usually learn the power swing first, and then instinctively continue to rotate their forearms when they learn to putt.

Either your forearms and putter face rotate through impact, or they don't. The greater the rotation, the less likely your putter will be square at impact.

Ball Position

There is a bottom (low point) to every arc, including that of the putting stroke. Position the low point of your stroke behind the ball, so it will launch putts slightly upward, rolling the ball on top of the grass.

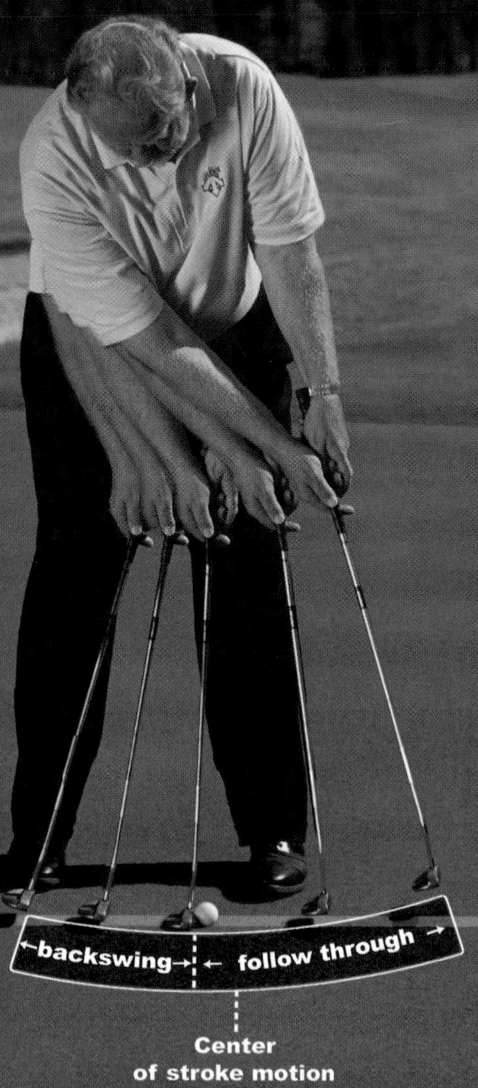

To insure a slightly upward angle of attack, perfect ball position is two inches ahead of the bottom of your stroke arc. For most golfers, this position is one ball-width behind the instep of the lead foot.

#6 Understand in your mind's eye: Spend 10 minutes reading and internalizing these statements. If you understand and believe them, you're done. If you have a problem with one of them, return to the relevant parts of the section above and study the figures and text until you don't:

1) Depending on how I hold the putter, where it is suspended from, and how long the shaft is, the putter face should not rotate at all, or just slightly, through the impact zone.
2) My hands and forearms should not rotate during the stroke.
3) My wrists should not hinge, and my body should not sway during my stroke.
4) The ball should be positioned about one ball inside my lead foot instep.

Posture, Alignment and Grip

In Chapter 1, I explained that having a clear vision of how you want to putt is critical to your improvement. Now I'll offer some examples to help build that vision. I'll begin with the set-up and posture of your body at address, how you hold what length of putter, what putting style you choose, and your flow-lines (the imaginary lines running through your shoulders, eyes and hips, indicating where your body is aiming).

Set-up and posture determine how a putter will swing naturally through impact. Since many golfers set-up with poor posture, poorly fit putters, and bad alignment, their only chance for success (by which I mean finding the hole, not making a good stroke) is to make in-stroke compensations. However, the greater the compensations, the less consistent the stroke. The following concepts will eliminate your need for in-stroke compensations.

Set-up in Good Posture

too upright

just right

too bent over

Look in a full-length mirror to determine the angle between your back (spine) and hips that feels best. There is no formula for this angle, and it can change (with age, a back problem, and so on). A good putting posture allows room for your hands and arms to hang naturally and swing past your body, your eyes to be vertically above the putt line, and your back to be comfortable.

If your back hurts when you putt, you'll never want to practice enough to be your best.

Your eyes should be vertically above your Aimline. If they aren't, your visual perception of the correct aim will change from putt to putt as the distance to the hole changes.

When your eyes are inside the Aimline, your visual aim angle changes with the length of each putt.The result? Inconsistent aim.

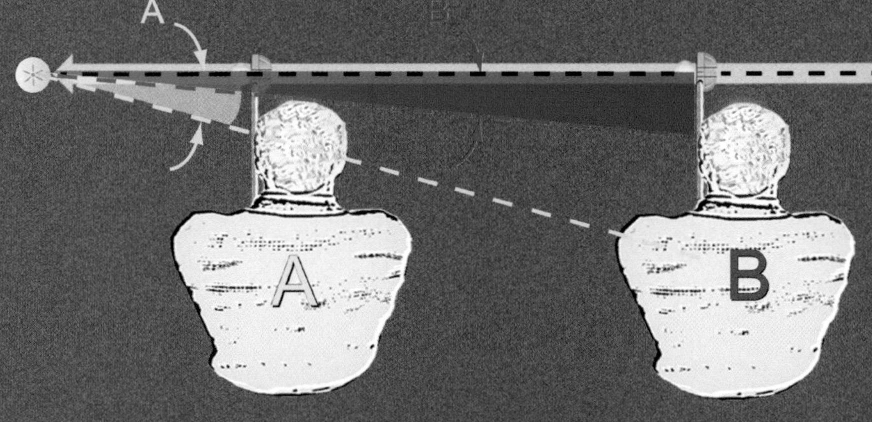

When your eyes are vertically above the Aimline, all visual aim angles are equal at 0 degrees. The result? Consistent aim.

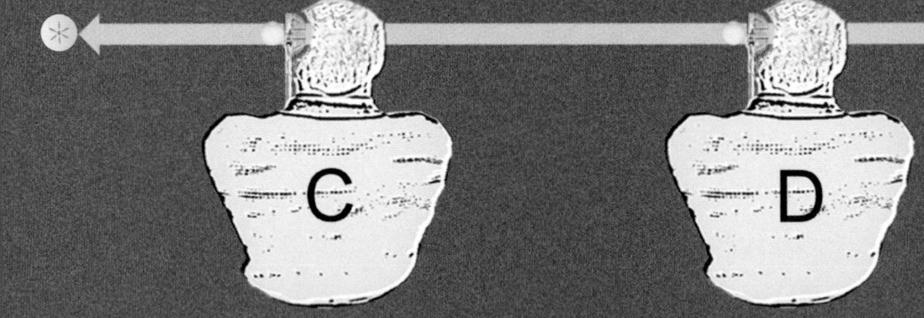

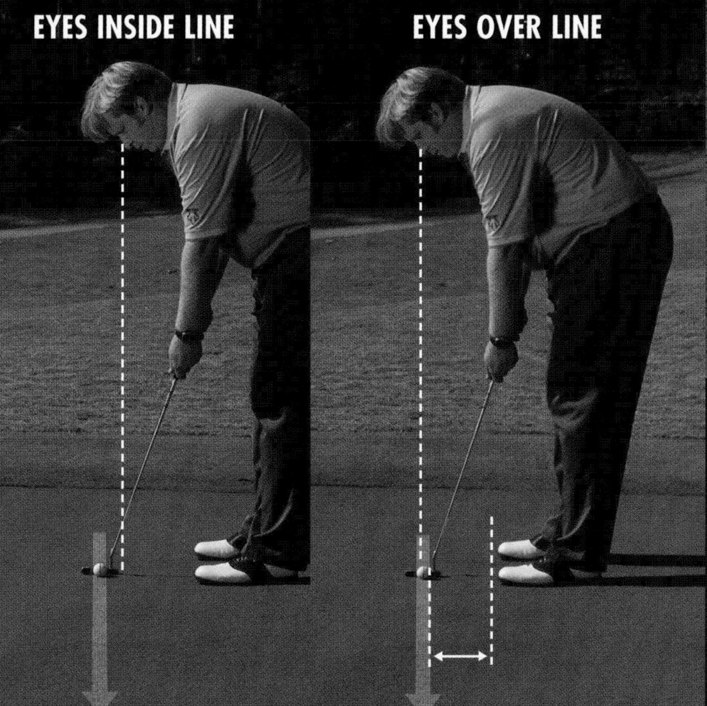

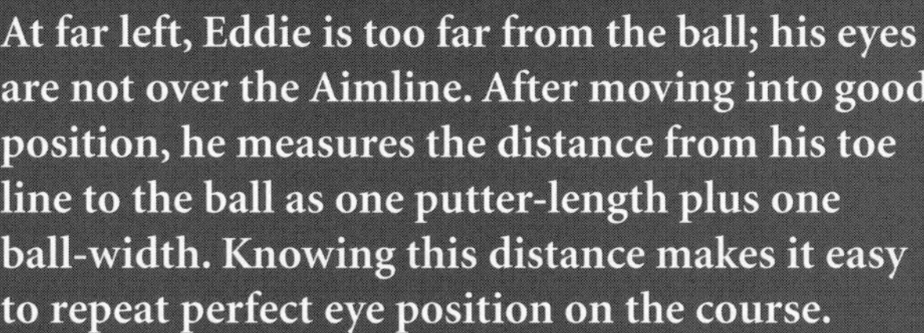

At far left, Eddie is too far from the ball; his eyes are not over the Aimline. After moving into good position, he measures the distance from his toe line to the ball as one putter-length plus one ball-width. Knowing this distance makes it easy to repeat perfect eye position on the course.

When putting with a body-anchor style (belly, chest, or neck), try to get your eyes directly over the Aimline. The closer your eyes are to vertically above the line, the better your ability to aim.

#7 Stand comfortably: Spend 10 minutes in front of a full-length mirror making sure you know the toe-line to ball distance that puts your eyes in the best position possible, without causing discomfort to your back. Write this distance down, because it's important. Maintain this distance for all future 10-Minute Sessions, and on the course, too.

Putter Fitting

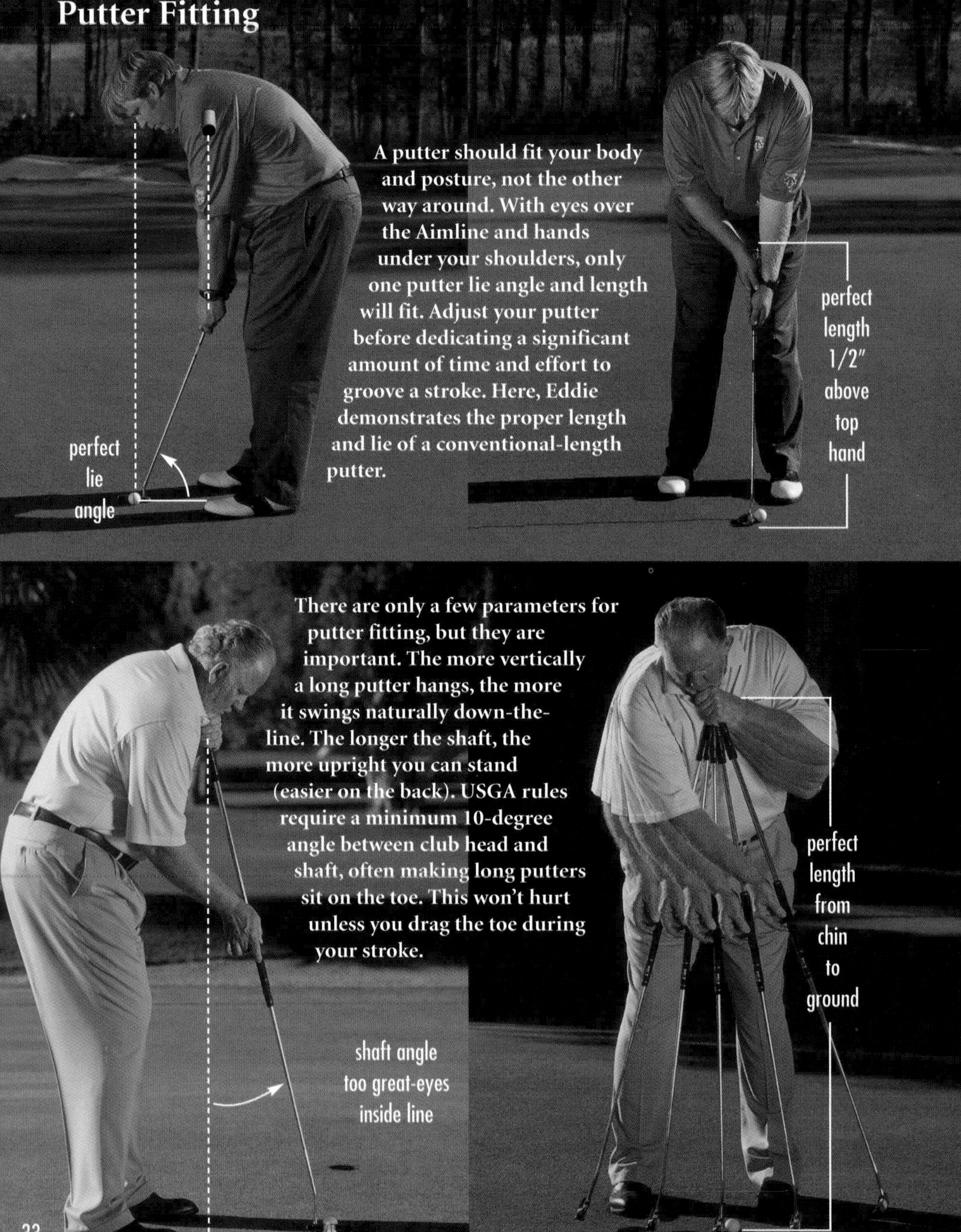

A putter should fit your body and posture, not the other way around. With eyes over the Aimline and hands under your shoulders, only one putter lie angle and length will fit. Adjust your putter before dedicating a significant amount of time and effort to groove a stroke. Here, Eddie demonstrates the proper length and lie of a conventional-length putter.

There are only a few parameters for putter fitting, but they are important. The more vertically a long putter hangs, the more it swings naturally down-the-line. The longer the shaft, the more upright you can stand (easier on the back). USGA rules require a minimum 10-degree angle between club head and shaft, often making long putters sit on the toe. This won't hurt unless you drag the toe during your stroke.

A body putter can be anchored on your body anywhere from your belly to your neck. You want the spot that is comfortable for your back and gives you good control. It can be held lead or trailing hand lowest on the grip. Just as with long putters, the body putter should swing as close to vertical as possible. This reduces face rotation through impact, and helps get your eyes closer to over the line for better aim.

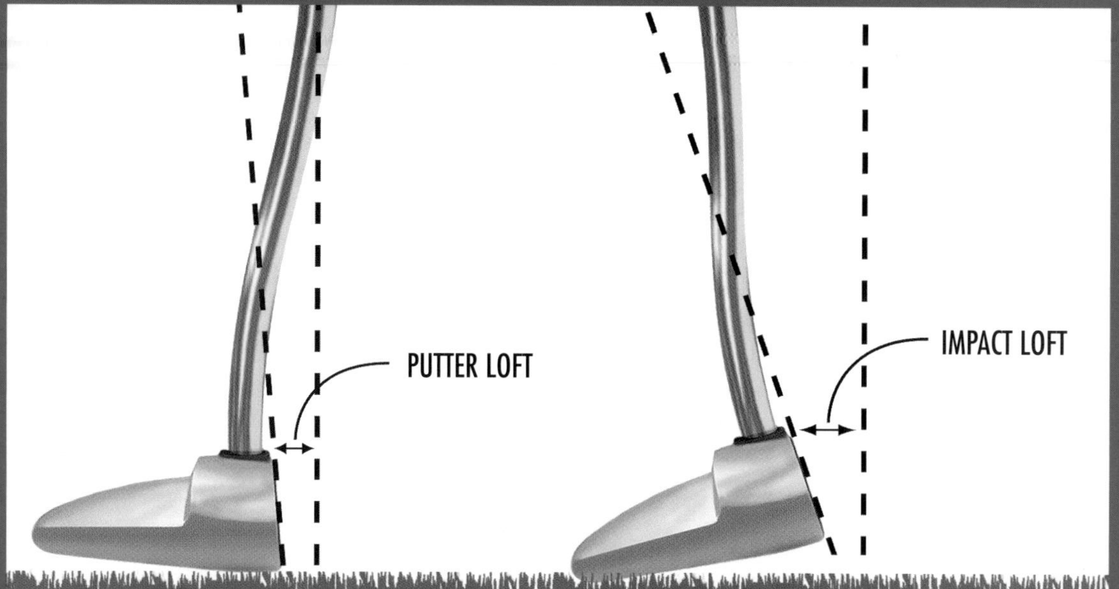

The putter loft is the angle between the face and the shaft. The impact loft angle is the face angle at impact, relative to vertical. Optimum impact angles vary from 1/4-degree on fast, hard-surfaced bent grass greens, to 4, 5, or even 6-degrees on soft, bumpy, Bermuda greens.

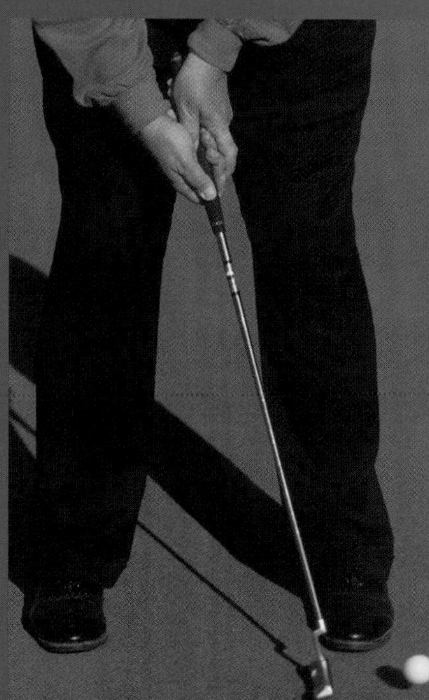

Impact loft can be very different from putter loft, depending on whether a player executes a hands-forward, hands-vertical, or hands-behind-putter-head position at impact. For consistent results, the hands should never be behind the ball at impact.

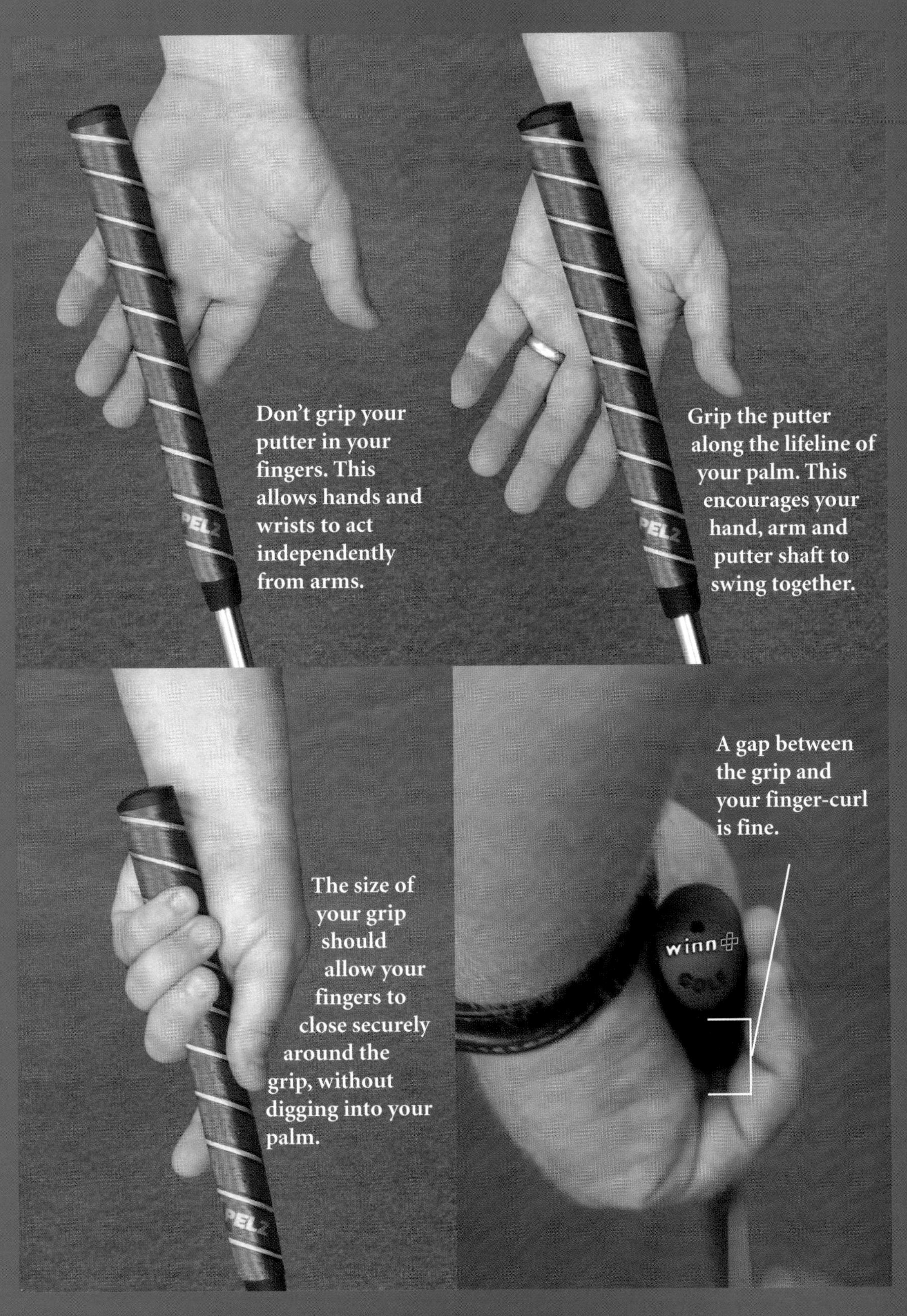
Don't grip your putter in your fingers. This allows hands and wrists to act independently from arms.
Grip the putter along the lifeline of your palm. This encourages your hand, arm and putter shaft to swing together.
The size of your grip should allow your fingers to close securely around the grip, without digging into your palm.
A gap between the grip and your finger-curl is fine.
winn

The grip shape should allow for consistent placement of your hands to accurately deliver your putter face squarely to impact. Know the shape that performs best for you, and its orientation relative to your putter face (flat on top shown here, perpendicular to putter face).

Installing a new grip rotated even a tiny bit off from the old one, means having to learn a new "square-at-impact" position for your hands. For this reason, I prefer wrap grips that come off and go on without changing the underlisting or its flat position.

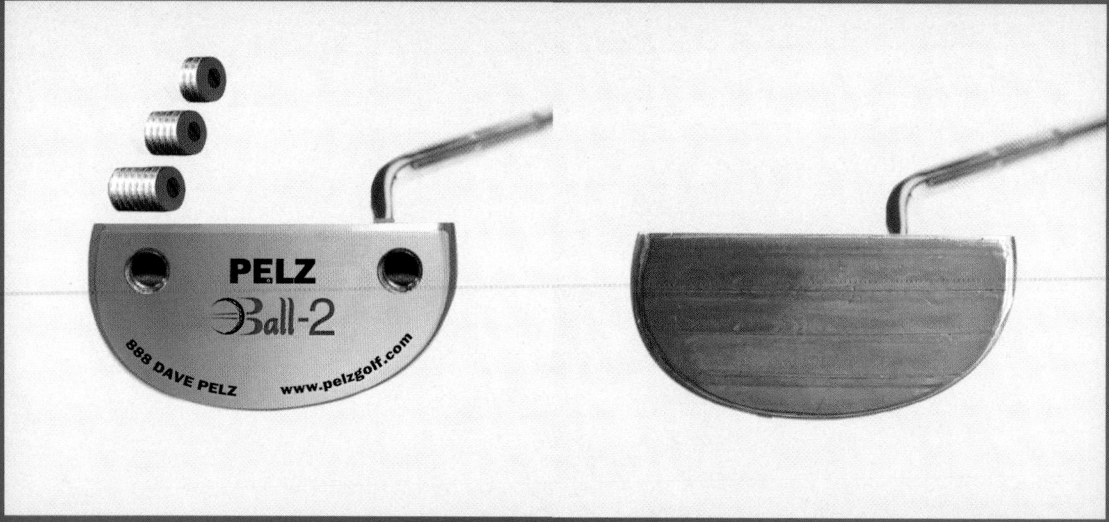

The weight of your putter head affects your touch and feel for distance. Adjust your putter's weight for optimum lag putting results. Head weight can be adjusted with weight plugs or lead tape.

All things being equal, the best putter-head shape for you is the one you aim the best (as long as it is properly fit for length, lie, loft, weight, and shaft axis location). The right putter should become "one" with you, in the correct posture, alignment, and grip position.

#8 Fall in Love with a Fitted Putter: It will take many 10-Minute Sessions and lots of experience to know which putter is best for you, but there is no rush. After you determine your putting style, get a putter that fits your body (length, lie, loft). See your golf professional, and evaluate all putters that fit. Stroke them, see how they feel and swing through impact (if you don't like how one feels, put it down.) Most important: Don't ever change your stroke or posture to fit a putter. If a putter doesn't fit...don't bother with it!

Aim your Flow Lines

Unless you manipulate the stroke, a putter swinging past the front of your body will move parallel to an imaginary line through your shoulders. The easiest way to execute a natural, non-manipulated stroke down the Aimline is to position your shoulder flow-lines parallel to it.

Good posture is simple: eyes over the Aimline, flow-lines parallel to that line. Conceptually simple yes, but "squaring up" is easier said than done. Golfers who say they feel square usually aren't, and when placed into square alignment, often say they don't feel right.

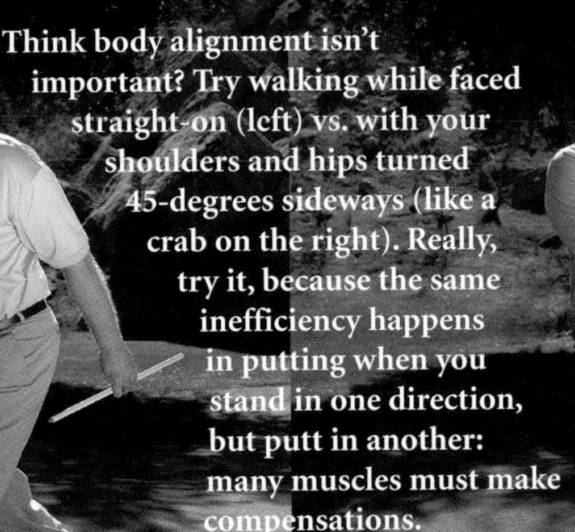

Think body alignment isn't important? Try walking while faced straight-on (left) vs. with your shoulders and hips turned 45-degrees sideways (like a crab on the right). Really, try it, because the same inefficiency happens in putting when you stand in one direction, but putt in another: many muscles must make compensations.

I'll never forget Steve Elkington struggling one day to "square-up" to his putts. After much effort and consternation, he stood up completely still for some time, then said, "Pelzie, if you'd just give me some #@ç!ing way to *seeeeee* my shoulder line, this would be a lot easier."

Thus, " Elk's Key®" was born, with lined mirrors to provide feedback on shoulder flow line alignment.

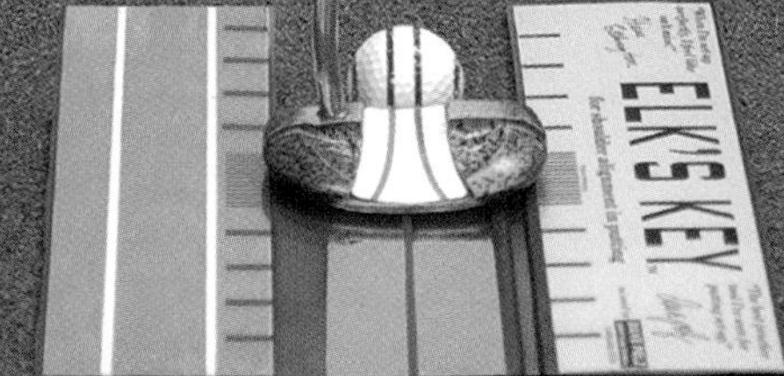

#9 Determine your address set-up: Set up to Elk's Key 25 times in 10 minutes. Align the mirror to a target (a tee or hole on the putting green, a soda can on a carpet at home), and address a ball as you aim at the target. Make sure the flow-lines of your eyes, toes, and shoulders are all parallel to the mirror lines every time. After every perfect set-up, putt the ball (using something indoors to deflect it, so the target doesn't move).

Develop a Square Grip at Impact

The grip is not supposed to make the ball go into the hole. The grip is supposed to enable your hands and arms to deliver your putter squarely to impact, with as much relaxation and as little pressure as possible. A good grip won't let the putter flop around or get ahead of or behind your hands, won't manipulate the putter face, and will never add or take energy out of your stroke. Ben Crenshaw grips it perfectly.

#10 Find your grip with no-hole, no-target putting: Without aiming at anything, set 3 O-Balls on a green or carpet with O-rings vertical. Address each ball with your putter square to the O-Ball lines and putt all three balls 10-feet or so, using your normal grip and stroke. Try to strike each ball squarely, so it rolls purely in its aim direction. It doesn't matter where or how far the balls roll. Simply watch to see how they roll: do the O-Balls show wobble or not? If they wobble, they were struck with side spin (putter face not square, or not moving along Aimline). If they don't wobble, it means your stroke was square and on line (O-Balls can't lie).

Your hand pressure should be light and passive through impact. There is no one grip perfect for all golfers, but there is a best grip for every individual. Find the one that most naturally delivers you're putter square at impact, and putt with it.

Now change your grip and putt again. Putt each set of three balls with a different grip and see which one produces the best, most consistently pure roll. In one 10-Minute Session, you can rule out several grips that won't work for you. In multiple 10-Minute Sessions, you can gain confidence in one grip above all the rest. Once you commit to the grip that delivers your best roll, all you have to learn is to aim it properly, and you're on your way.

3 Putting Procedures

With a solid mental foundation and a clear understanding of the fundamental concepts of your putting game from the first two chapters, the next step in improving is to establish an environment in which you can imbed your stroke mechanics so they will be repeatable and usable when you need them. The best way to do this is to establish a procedure you follow consistently both before and after every putt that not only allows you, but also helps prepare you, to make the best stroke you have in you, every time.

The optimum procedure consists of a putting routine and ritual, two different procedures that you conduct in your natural body rhythm, so that they surround and become a part of your putting stroke. The better you develop your routine and ritual, the easier it will be to imbed your stroke into it, and the better your results will be.

Putting Routine

Before every putt, you read the green (green-reading is discussed in Chapter 6). During the actual act of putting, you execute your ritual and your stroke. Everything else–how you prepare yourself physically, mentally, and emotionally to execute the best stroke you can, and then the analysis of both what you and your ball did–is your putting routine.

A routine, composed of pre- and post-putt segments, does not include making judgments on the slope, the speed of the green, or how much break to play. Those are all part of green-reading. The pre-putt routine starts after you've decided what the perfect roll of your putt should look like, and helps you determine what to do to make that roll happen. It includes your practice strokes and your set-up and alignment, everything up until you start your putting ritual and stroke. A post-putt routine (which most golfers don't have) should consist of a quick evaluation of your stroke and its results. The post-putt routine is important because learning from your current putts will benefit your future putting.

Use the Same Routine

Mike Weir practices before the tournament each week. When professionals practice, they prepare for how they will putt in the tournament. They never want to face performing something for the first time, when it really counts.

Mike putts in tournaments like he putts in practice. Your pre- and post-putt routines should be the same whether you are rolling practice putts or making the most important putt of your career. The more closely your practice resembles your play and you play the way you've practiced, the better you will perform under pressure.

6-Step Putting Routine

See it

Read Green
- Putt distance, Speed of green
- Slope (down, up, side hill)
- Grain, Wind, Moisture

1. Imagine Perfect Ball Track
- Stand Behind ball on Aimline
- Eyes horizontal (use binocular vision)
- 3 preliminary practice swings

Feel it

2. Walk to Your Ball
- Internalize Aimline in mind/body
- Feel slope under feet

3. Set-Up to Imaginary Ball (4" inside)
- Flowlines parallel - left of Aimline

4. Practice Swings: Create Preview Stroke
- 3 Strokes minimum - 6 maximum
- Imagine perfect speed 17" roll past hole
- Commit to feel and minds eye vision of perfect preview stroke

Do it

5. Move into Final Address Position
- Eyes over Aimline (exact toe to ball distance)
- One look to verify proper alignment
- Pull the trigger to initiate putting ritual

Execute Ritual - Stroke Putt

Learn from it

6. Hold Finish
- Evaluate quality of roll (0-Ball wobble)
- Evaluate speed (17" past)
- Evaluate green read (if roll & speed good)

Step 1 of your routine starts from 6 feet behind the ball, standing on the Aimline, after reading the green. Look out past your ball (keep your eyes horizontal, so to use binocular vision) and imagine how you expect it to roll along the perfect ball track into the hole. If your imagination is vivid enough, ghosted balls will seem to appear on the real green, but will actually be in your mind's eye.

You know how much break to play, and you've seen the imaginary ball track. Now make three preliminary practice swings–each one relaxed and casual–that you think might work for this putt. Think of this as creating a draft swing for an initial evaluation. Look at the hole on draft swing #1, at the ball on draft swing #2, then back at the hole on #3. Don't work too hard on making this swing feel perfect; it's just to get you in the mood for the serious work ahead.

Feel It

Step 2 is to walk to the ball along the Aimline, trying to keep your eyes above it. Internalize this Aimline into your mind and body because it is where you are going to aim your putter and your stroke, and where you want to start the putt.

4 inches

Step 3 is to address an imaginary ball 4-inches inside the real ball.

Next imagine rolling the imaginary ball over an imaginary hole just to the left of the real hole.

<u>Step 4</u> **is to make a practice stroke and feel if it's the right size to roll the imaginary ball 17 inches past the imaginary hole. This stroke feels too short.**

The next practice swing feels too long, like it might roll the putt too far past the hole.

Take another practice swing, then another, and, if necessary, another until you feel the perfect swing to roll the imaginary putt the perfect distance at the perfect speed. Having felt the perfect stroke, you've created a preview of the real stroke needed to make the real ball roll into the real hole.

Do It

Step 5 is to move in to your real address position, take one look to make sure you are ready to go, and pull the trigger (see page 54) on your putting ritual and stroke.

#11 Build your routine: Away from the golf course, at home or in your office, write down what you are going to do before and after every putt in your putting routine. Then execute this routine a few times with a putter, but no ball. Place a quarter on the carpet to represent the ball, a soda can for the cup. Start from behind the ball (step #1), proceed through your practice strokes, move in, putting the real ball (quarter), and

Learn From It

Step 6 is to hold your finish position as you watch and learn from your stroke and putt. Watching your putts roll while the feel and vision of your stroke are still strong, will teach you three things: 1) If the ball rolled purely, 2) If it rolled the correct speed, and 3) If you read the correct amount of break.

To optimize feedback, keep your body as still as possible, simply turning your head to watch the ball and correlate the result with your feel. Small (less than 1/4-inch) differences in 10-foot putts can make tremendous differences in putting. You need to learn the feel of stroke changes that cause these differences.

hold your stroke finish while watching the putt roll (step #6). Run through your entire pre- and post-putt routine at least 15 times so you'll be sure to remember it the next time you go to the course. Then use it for the rest of your golfing career.

Putting Ritual

A putting ritual is a sequence of motions that establishes your body rhythm before and through your stroke, and continues to the holding of your finish. The ritual consists of several rhythmic physical motions to set the cadence (page 65) for your pre-stroke ritual, the stroke itself, plus your stroke finish. A good ritual must be simple enough and rhythmic enough to let the golfer get into it (after practicing it many times, it should become a habit) and execute the complete putting stroke without thinking about the mechanics.

The ritual also should take less than 8-seconds, so the feel and image of the golfer's preview stroke is not diminished or lost prior to putting. The stroke motions back and through are part of the putting ritual. They should always happen at the same rhythm, in the same time, and in the same sequence, so they can become automatic and repeatable (especially under pressure, when the mind is racing and thinking about extraneous things).

Features of the Ritual

1. Composed of visible body motions - cannot be mental.

2. Every motion coincides with a beat of your body rhythm cadence (page 65), the same as the "tick-tock" of your practice strokes.

3. Back swing and through swing occur on beats, and are part of ritual.

4. Rhythm matched to players natural body rhythm, the same for all length strokes and putts.

5. Takes less than 8 seconds, preview stroke to impact.

Find a Trigger to Start Your Ritual

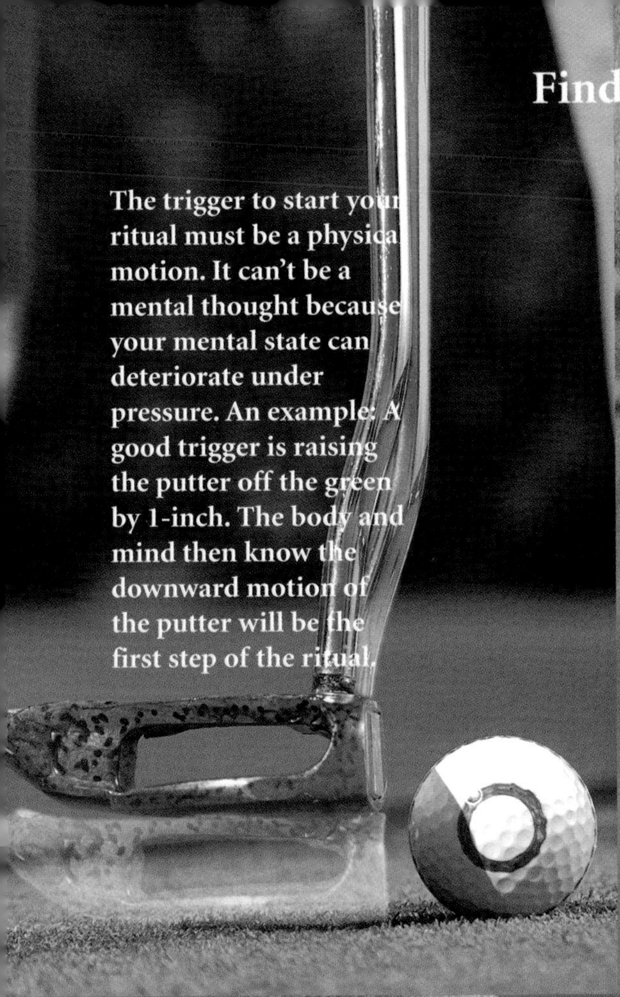

The trigger to start your ritual must be a physical motion. It can't be a mental thought because your mental state can deteriorate under pressure. An example: A good trigger is raising the putter off the green by 1-inch. The body and mind then know the downward motion of the putter will be the first step of the ritual.

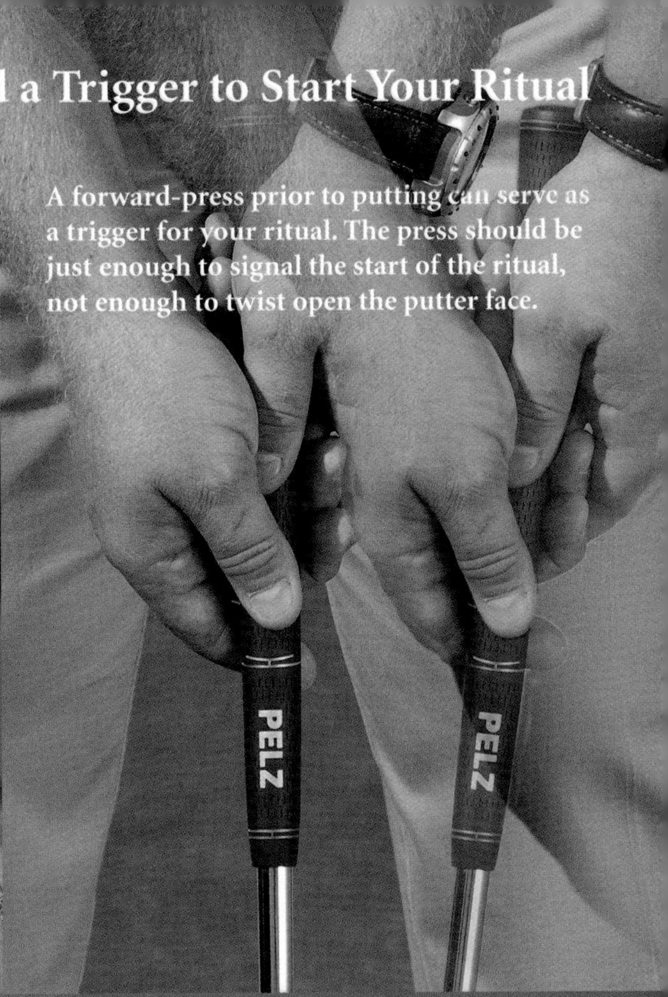

A forward-press prior to putting can serve as a trigger for your ritual. The press should be just enough to signal the start of the ritual, not enough to twist open the putter face.

Another example: Start the ritual by lifting your thumb on a beat of your body rhythm (details on page 64). The first count of your ritual then becomes returning the thumb to the grip.

Develop Your Ritual

UP

DOWN

LOOK

LOOK

BACK

THROUGH

HOLD

WATCH

Your ritual must be in sync with the cadence of your body rhythm; one move for every count and every move must be physical (page 65 for rhythm). My ritual marches to a count of 7, with my putter pick-up triggering the start.

Count #1: I lightly touch my putter down on the green surface (no pressure).

Count #2: I look down the Aimline, not to see anything, just to establish my rhythm with a head movement.

Count #3: I look back to the ball, making another head movement to keep my rhythm going.

Count #4: I take my backswing (remember, the stroke is part of my putting ritual).

Count #5: My stroke through impact occurs at the count of 5.

Count #6: I hold my finish for one count; just to make sure I finish my stroke completely.

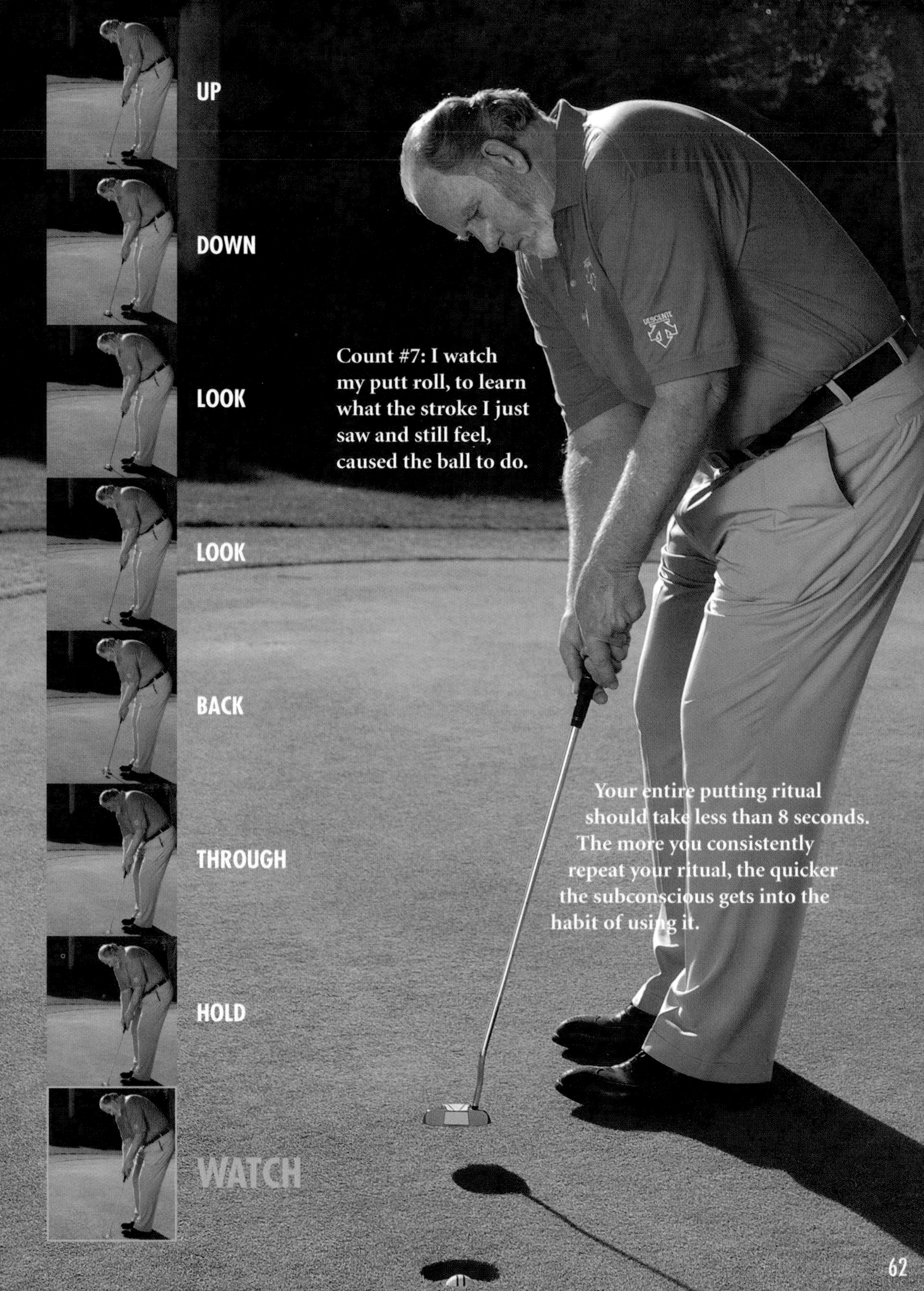

Count #7: I watch my putt roll, to learn what the stroke I just saw and still feel, caused the ball to do.

Your entire putting ritual should take less than 8 seconds. The more you consistently repeat your ritual, the quicker the subconscious gets into the habit of using it.

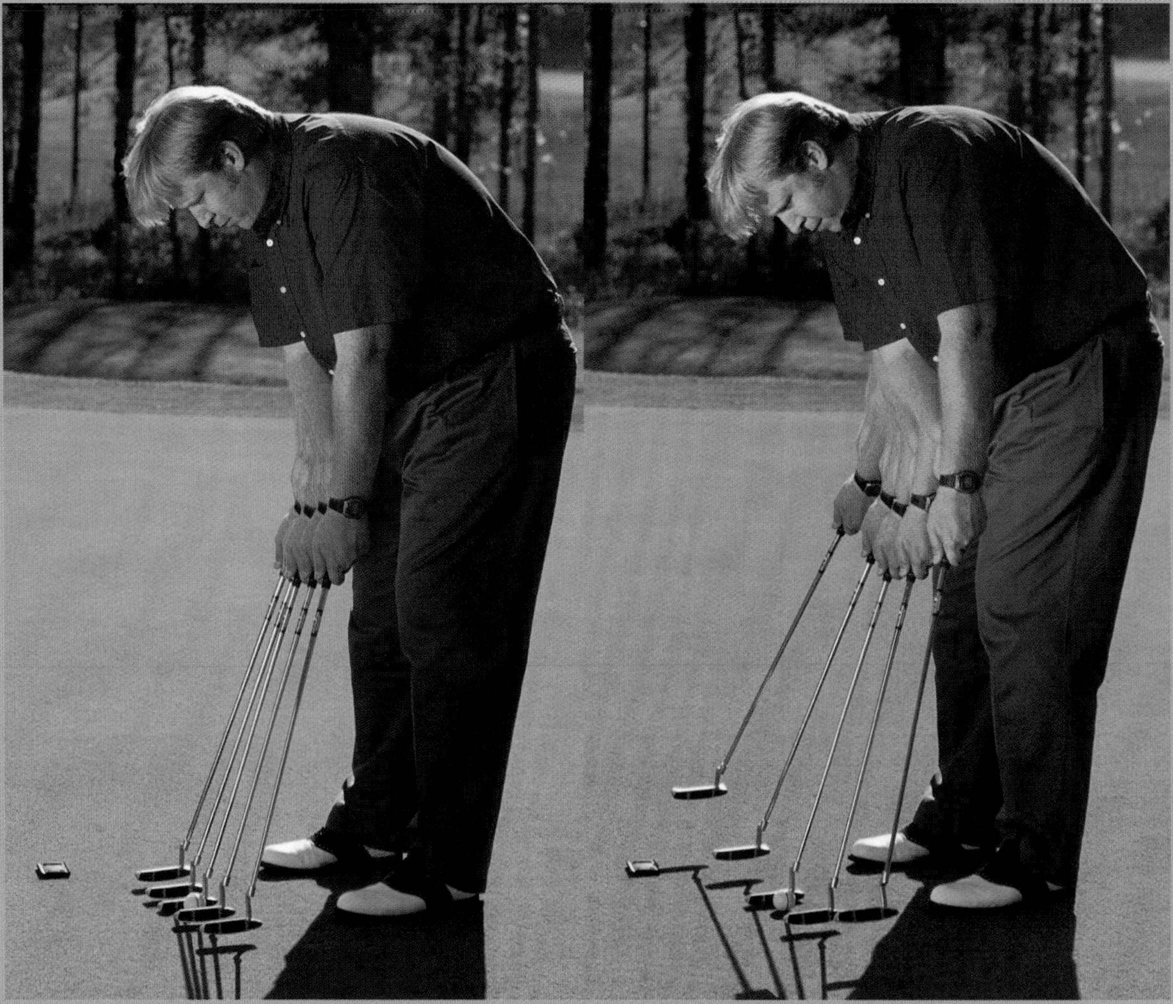

Always use the same stroke ritual cadence no matter how long the putt. Eddie strokes a 3-foot putt (left) and a 30-footer (right). He uses the same ritual and rhythm for both. Our section on how to find the cadence that works best for you starts on the facing page.

#12 Build your Ritual: After developing a comfortable ritual at home, you must validate that it works on the course before you totally accept it. Take it to the practice putting green and use it on both long and short putts to make sure it is comfortable. Imagine (pretend) you are facing the most important putt of your life and you want to use this ritual. If you like what you feel, write down the steps so they are easy to remember until they become part of you. (Don't forget to build in holding your finish and analyzing your results, so you can learn from every bit of feedback available).

Rhythm

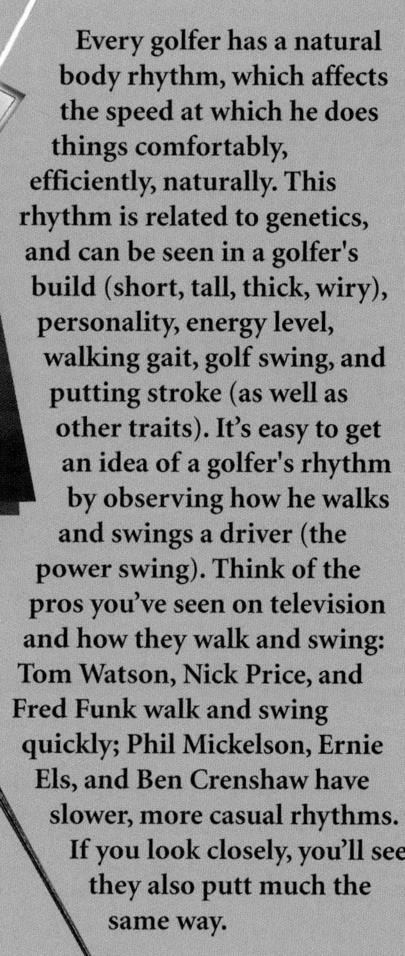

Every golfer has a natural body rhythm, which affects the speed at which he does things comfortably, efficiently, naturally. This rhythm is related to genetics, and can be seen in a golfer's build (short, tall, thick, wiry), personality, energy level, walking gait, golf swing, and putting stroke (as well as other traits). It's easy to get an idea of a golfer's rhythm by observing how he walks and swings a driver (the power swing). Think of the pros you've seen on television and how they walk and swing: Tom Watson, Nick Price, and Fred Funk walk and swing quickly; Phil Mickelson, Ernie Els, and Ben Crenshaw have slower, more casual rhythms. If you look closely, you'll see they also putt much the same way.

Find Your Body-Rhythm

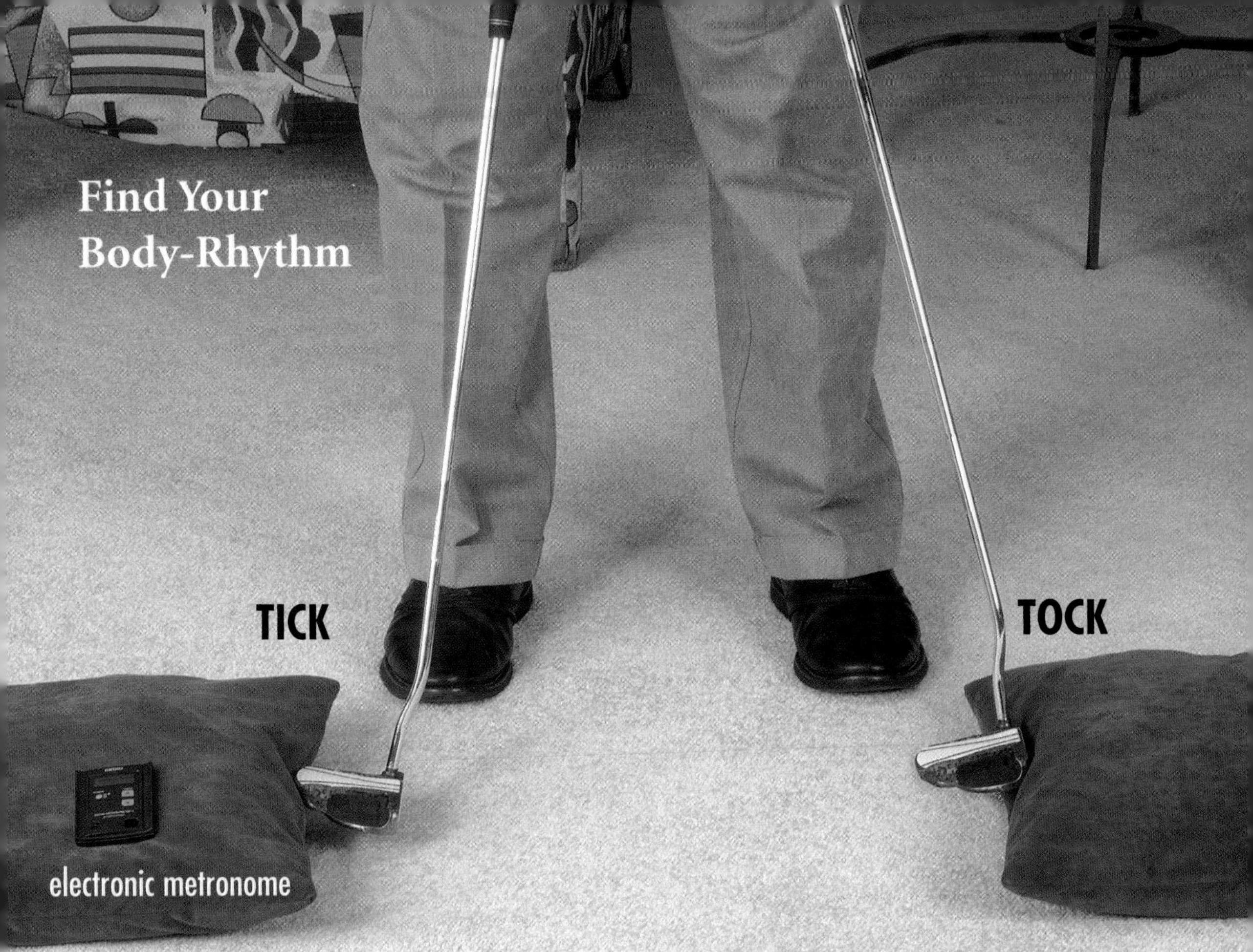

TICK

TOCK

electronic metronome

Your body will swing the putter most efficiently and comfortably at your natural body rhythm. Once you find it, putt with it for the rest of your career.

#13 Find Your Natural Rhythm: To find your natural body rhythm, start with a metronome ticking at 90 beats per minute and two pillows 18-inches apart. Move your putter in rhythm, touching one pillow on every beat, tick tock, tick tock, tick tock, back forth, back forth, back forth. Close your eyes and concentrate on how much effort it takes to swing your putter at that rhythm.

Reset the metronome 5 beats faster and do the test again. Repeat (always with your eyes shut) at faster and slower rates until you feel your easiest, most natural stroke rhythm. Finding your best rhythm may take just one 10-Minute Session or several sessions, several nights in a row. Just don't give up, because finding your body rhythm is very important.

Go to the course with a metronome and execute your putting stroke ritual for long and short putts. Try a 2-foot putt, then immediately stroke a 30-footer at the same rhythm. If both the long and short putts don't feel comfortable, you've yet to find your natural rhythm. Every golfer has a single rhythm that works best for all length putts.

4 Groove Good Stroke Mechanics

To putt well, golfers know they need a good stroke, so that's what they think they need to work on. But most don't realize that stroke mechanics also need to become part of their sub-conscious control, so they can be executed without having to think how or what must be done.

This chapter will show you how to learn a good stroke, one that starts with good aim, then adds accurate power, a precision face angle, solid ball contact, and a well-aligned motion through impact, to produce putts that roll on-line at the right speed. But while stroke mechanics are important to optimum putting performance, you can't think about what

you're doing as you are doing it. Putting strokes are too complicated to think your way through. You must train yourself to make them out of *habit*.

Putting is not about thinking. The ball never cares what you think about, it cares only about how you move your putter through impact and the conditions of the greens. By developing and grooving good stroke mechanics, then internalizing them so they become sub-consciously controlled habits, you can focus on *seeing* (reading where to aim) and *making* putts when you get to the course.

Putter Aim and Body Alignment

A golfer's perception of his putter and body alignment is often far from reality. He aims the putter first, then sets his body and stroke relative to that direction. So Putter Aim is the first fundamental of stroke mechanics, because it occurs first, and affects everything that follows.

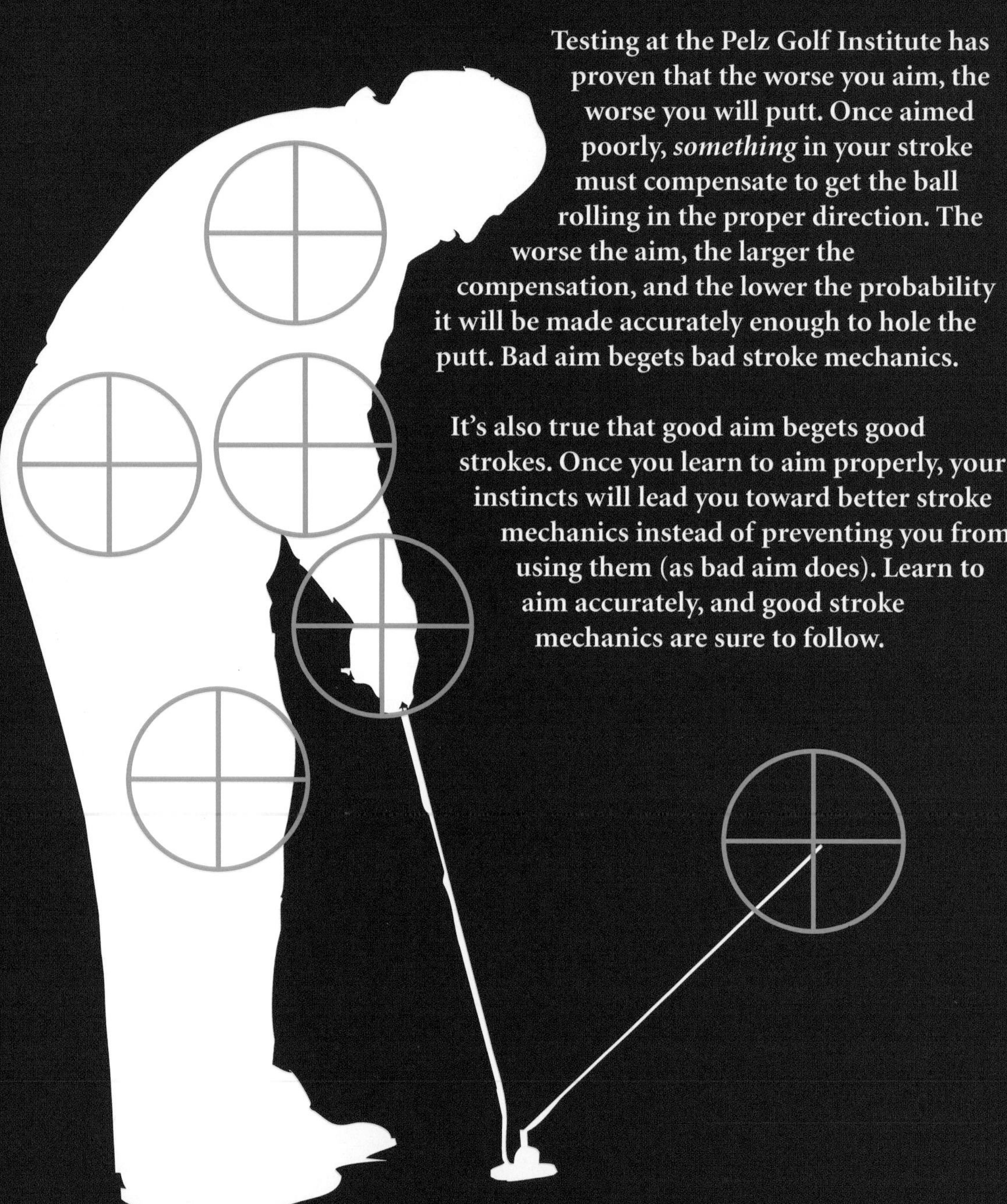

Testing at the Pelz Golf Institute has proven that the worse you aim, the worse you will putt. Once aimed poorly, *something* in your stroke must compensate to get the ball rolling in the proper direction. The worse the aim, the larger the compensation, and the lower the probability it will be made accurately enough to hole the putt. Bad aim begets bad stroke mechanics.

It's also true that good aim begets good strokes. Once you learn to aim properly, your instincts will lead you toward better stroke mechanics instead of preventing you from using them (as bad aim does). Learn to aim accurately, and good stroke mechanics are sure to follow.

Seeing Good Aim

If your first 1,000 putts were made with a pointer on your putter, chances are you would have seen and learned good aim from the start. But most golfers have no feedback device for aim, so if they miss putts to the left, they instinctively begin aiming to the right while convincing themselves that they are aiming better. Conversely, golfers who naturally push putts to the right learn to aim left. Research shows that from 10 feet, only 1 in 10 golfers aims the putter within two inches of where he is trying to aim. That is a serious handicap in putting, since the hole is only 4.25-inches wide!

The Pointer™ helps our students see proper putter aim.

The Pointer™ is especially effective on short putts. Find a dead-straight 3-footer and try putting to the left edge until several lip-out. Then try the same thing at the right edge. Having lipped-out on both edges makes holing putts in the center much easier.

#14 Seeing Good Aim: On a practice green, place five tees behind a hole so they are spaced at the inside left edge, left center, center, right center, and inside right edge. Locate a straight, 3-footer to that hole and with a Pointer on your putter face, try to hole three putts aiming at each tee. Finish the session by taking the Pointer off your putter and holing 15 more putts aiming at the same tees. This session will improve your vision for detail in aiming.

Align Your Body

Many golfers stand open to their Aimline (flow lines aligned left), hoping it will help them see the line better. Unfortunately this makes swinging the putter down the line more difficult.

A better set-up is to align your body flow lines parallel to your Aimline. "See" your Aimline from behind the putt, then learn to aim your putter and align your body down that line.

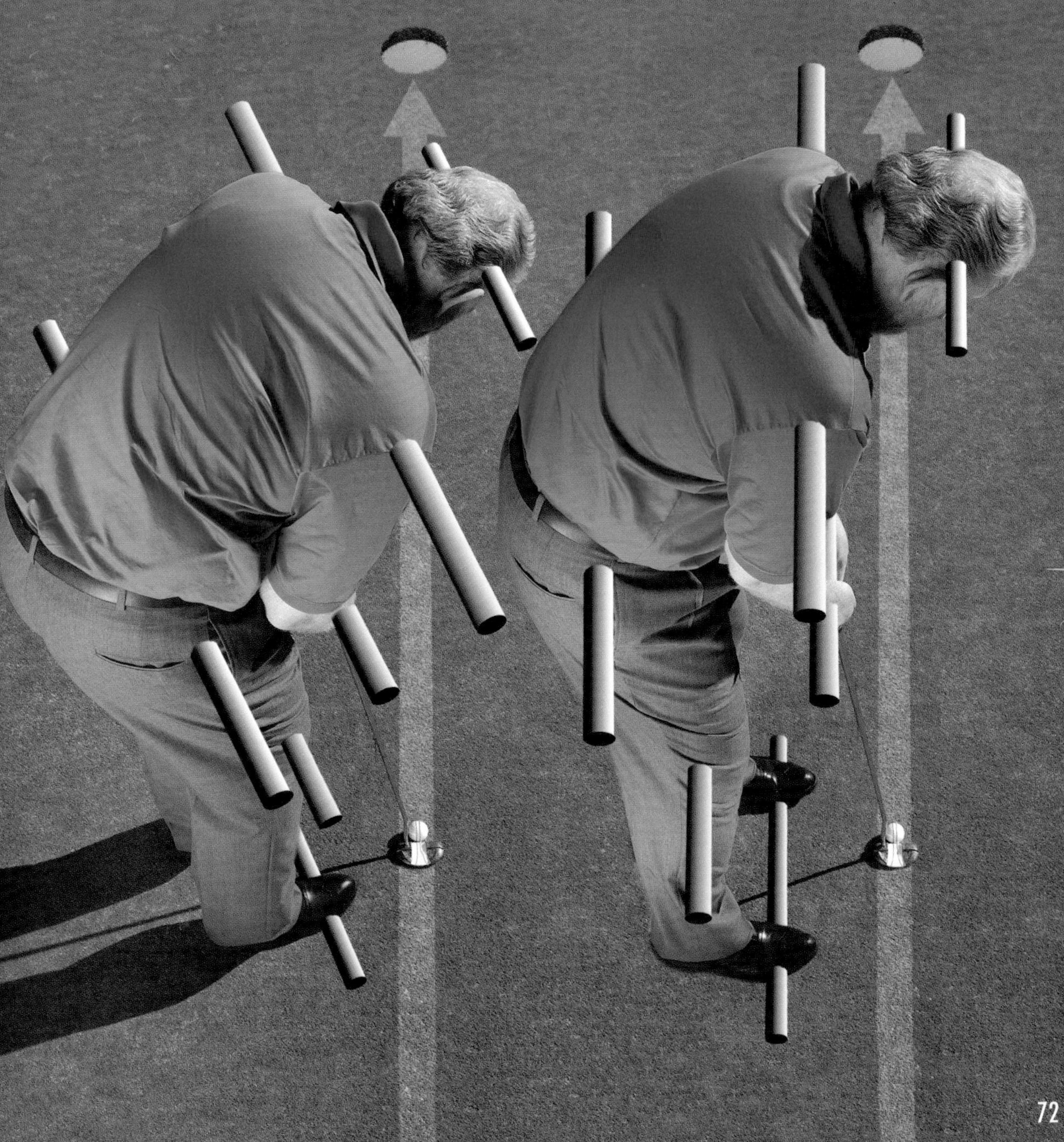

Elk's Key® provides visual feedback on putter aim, as well as the flow lines of the shoulders and eyes relative to the Aimline.

Shoulders: OPEN

Shoulders: PARALLEL

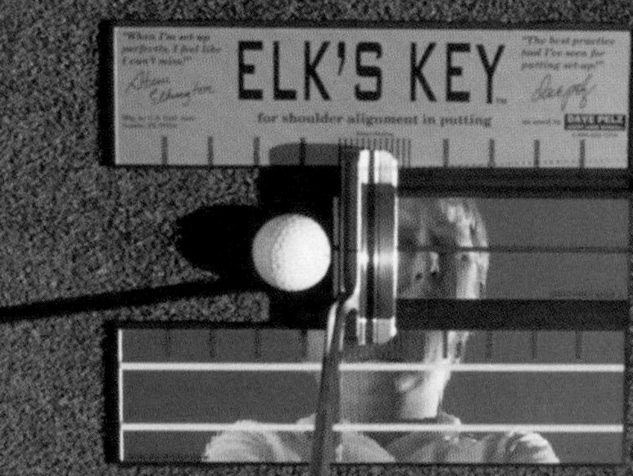

#15 Learn the Feel of the Perfect Set-up: On your home carpet, aim Elk's Key at a bottle or can and roll 40 6-foot putts. Deflect the putts so you aren't worried about moving the target. Focus on your eyes, feet, and shoulder alignment lines all being parallel to the Aimline, as you re-address each putt. Alternate this session with one on the practice green, trying to hole all 40 putts.

Learn Pure Aim Indoors

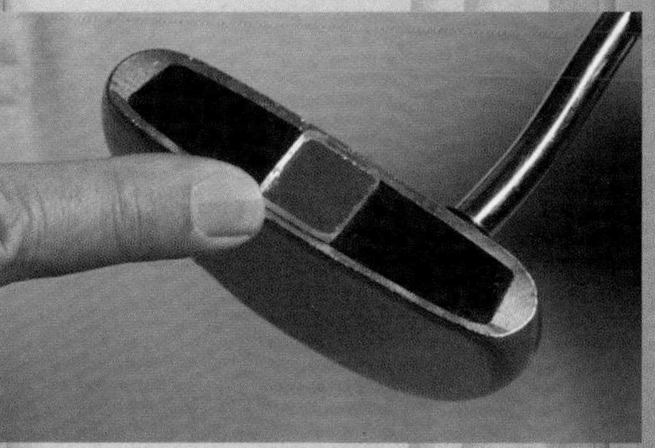

The LazrAimer™ bounces a low-power laser beam off a Plexiglas mirror taped to the putter face. The reflected beam provides golfers with immediate, accurate, and reliable feedback on aim.

Aim your putter at the LazrAimer (as if it were a hole) from three different distances. Once aimed, hold the putter still and voice-activate the laser beam by saying "On." The beam will bounce off your putter face to the wall behind the LazrAimer, showing you the quality of your aim (right, left, or perfect).

#16 Ingrain the Look of Perfect Aim: Practicing indoors, aim at the LazrAimer 5 times from each of 3 different distances. Back away and re-set your address position each time. You will improve rapidly in each session, but will regress between sessions. Repeat this session until your initial attempts in each session indicate good aim.

Aim your O-Ball™

Aiming an O-Ball™ at the right edge of the hole helps a golfer commit to that line.

O-Balls can also help line up a putter accurately to the same Aimline.

Watching O-Balls roll gives feedback on your putting stroke. O-Balls exhibit pure roll (no wobble) when stroked precisely on-line without sidespin. Good (but not quite perfect) strokes produce a slight wobble, medium strokes show medium wobble, and bad strokes equal bad wobble.

No wobble, good stroke, good read

No wobble, good stroke, bad read

Bad wobble, bad stroke, no feedback on read

No info on stroke from ordinary balls

#17 Aim and Putt with O-Balls™: O-Balls were developed at the Pelz Golf Institute to help golfers aim and putt better. The only drawback to using O-Balls is the time it takes to aim properly before each putt (gets easier and quicker with practice), and they can look funny on fairway shots (can't be re-aligned). To evaluate if O-Balls help you, align an O-Ball before each putt on a practice green for one 10-Minute Session, and watch them roll. This will acclimate you to the stroke feedback they provide. Then play an O-Ball for several rounds on the course. If you putt better, use O-Balls all the time.

Reality Check Your Aim

Do your putts start where you aim? The Putting Tutor® will tell you. A plastic platform with a cleat underneath, it sticks to a green or carpet on the spot you want to putt from. Rotate the small end to aim directly down your Aimline.

Looking from the hole back to the ball, the Tutor's two brass marbles form a gate along the Aimline, telling you when putts start off line.

When your stroke starts putts off line, the Tutor notifies you immediately by means of gate marble motion.

The Tutor verifies when your stroke starts the ball on-line (putts roll cleanly through marble gate), allowing you to see how good your aim was.

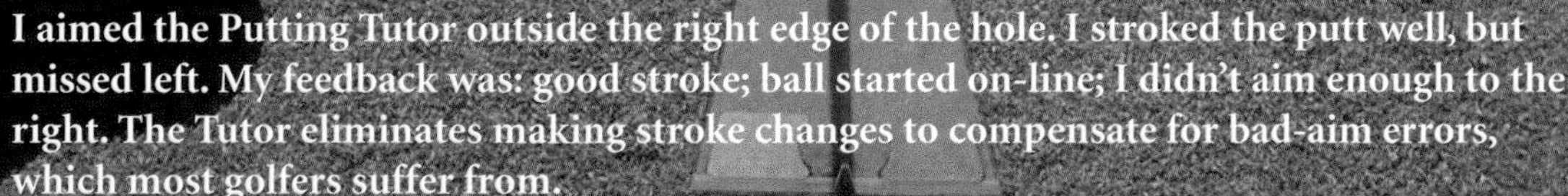

I aimed the Putting Tutor outside the right edge of the hole. I stroked the putt well, but missed left. My feedback was: good stroke; ball started on-line; I didn't aim enough to the right. The Tutor eliminates making stroke changes to compensate for bad-aim errors, which most golfers suffer from.

A putter aimed right of Aimline looks open

The back edge of the Tutor shows square alignment

A putter aimed left looks obviously closed

The marble gate has three settings (standard, pro, super-pro). The tighter the tolerance, the more accurate the feedback on your starting line.

#18 Reality Check Your Aim and Starting Line: The Putting Tutor always shows where you are aiming and how you start putts relative to that line. Putt 25 putts in each 10-Minute Session, with this feedback. Start at a gate tolerance where you are successful at least 50% of the time. Once you can roll approximately 80% of your putts through the gates, move to the next tighter tolerance.

Power Source

The power source of your stroke affects your ability to control the speed of your putts, which has a major influence on your success. A putt's speed affects how much it breaks, the line it rolls on, and whether or not it stays in the hole if it hits it. So how you supply power and speed is important.

Good putters need a gentle, precise, repeatable, reliable-under-pressure, easily adjustable, and finely controllable source of power. What they don't want is a powerful, fast, sporadic, explosive-under-pressure, susceptible-to-excitement-and-adrenaline source of power. In this section, you'll learn about your stroke's power source (or sources), and whether you need to modify and improve it.

Measure Where Your Power Comes From

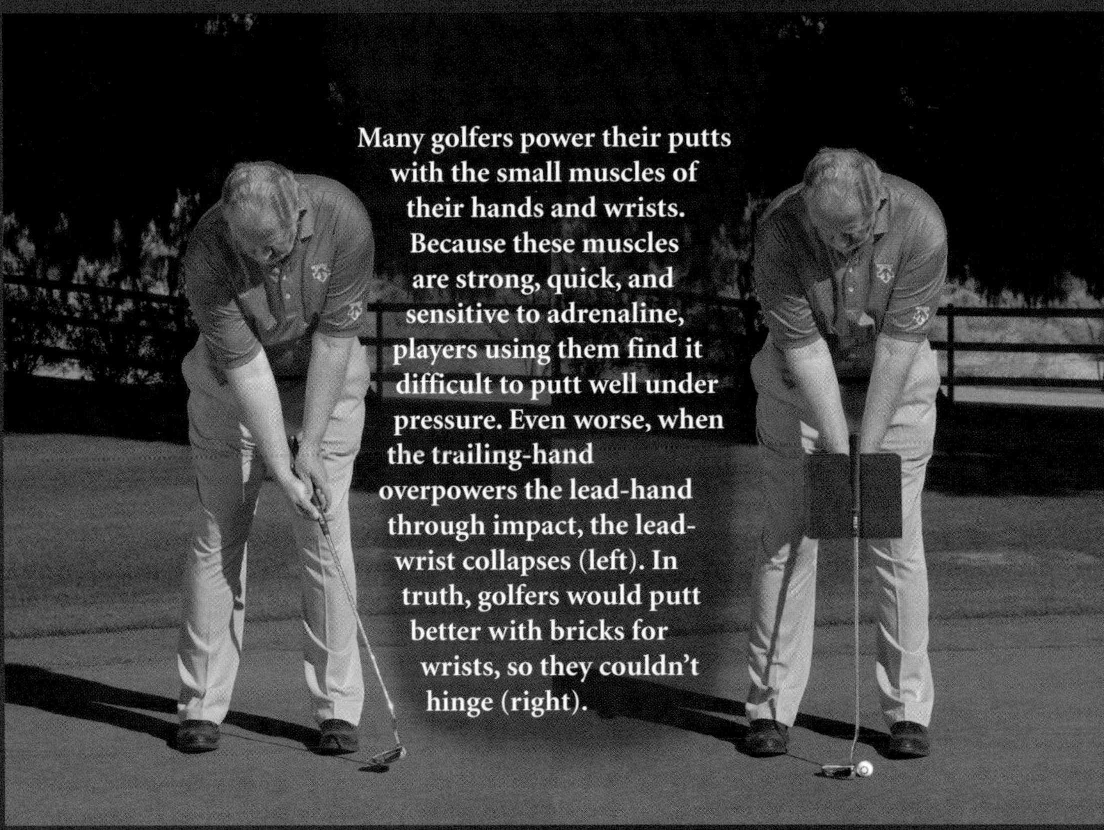

Many golfers power their putts with the small muscles of their hands and wrists. Because these muscles are strong, quick, and sensitive to adrenaline, players using them find it difficult to putt well under pressure. Even worse, when the trailing-hand overpowers the lead-hand through impact, the lead-wrist collapses (left). In truth, golfers would putt better with bricks for wrists, so they couldn't hinge (right).

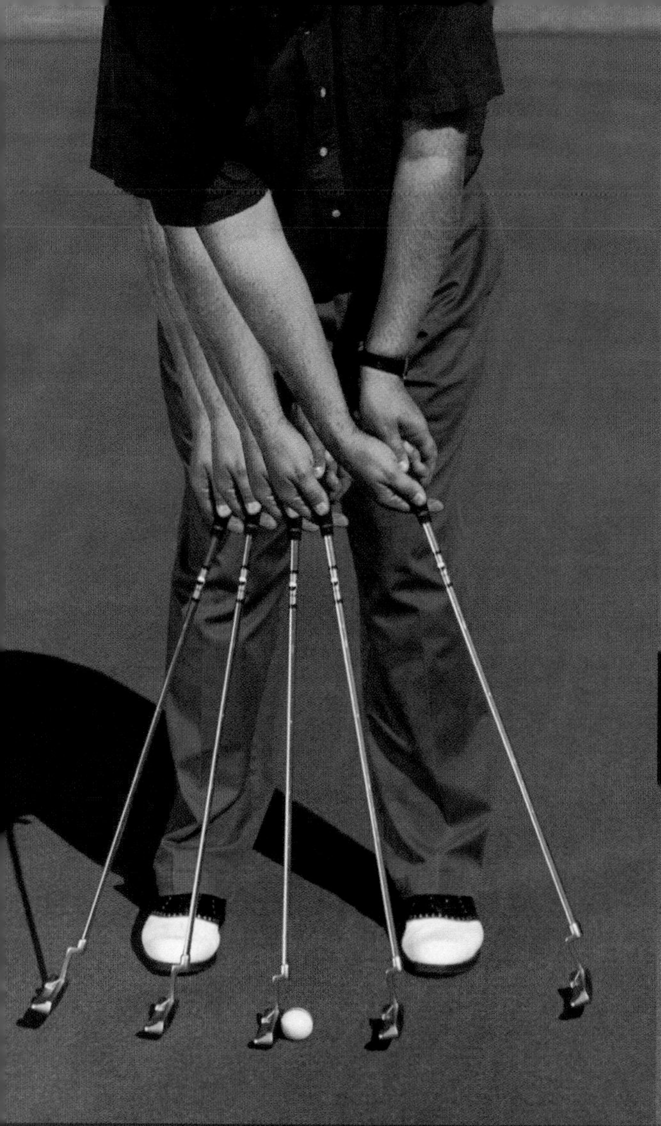

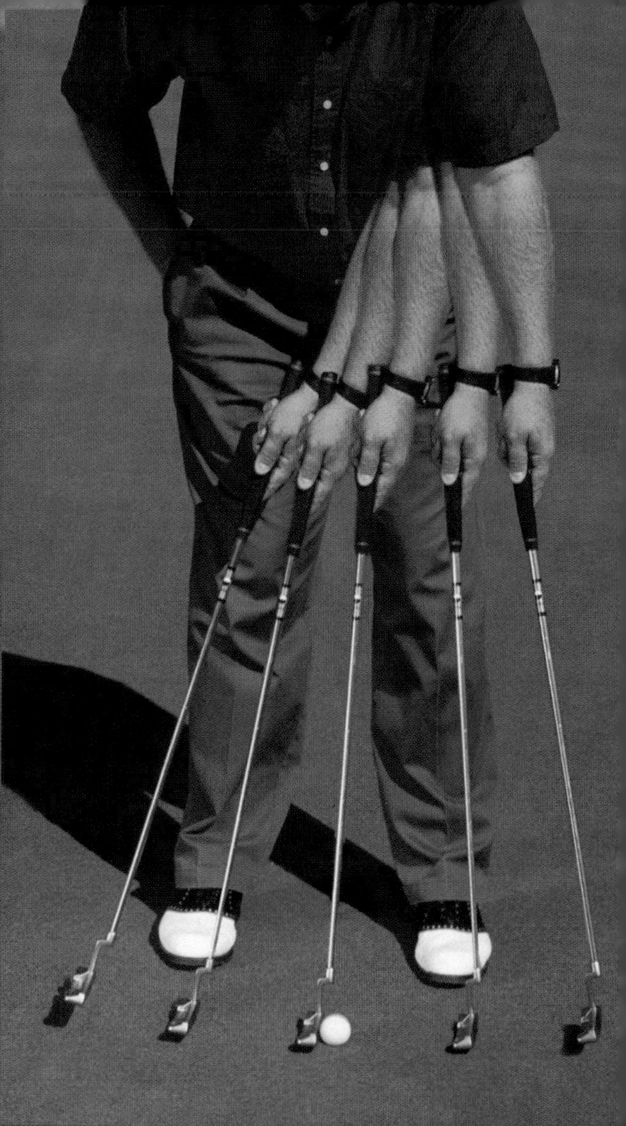

Take your normal grip and putt until you make a 10-foot putt at good speed. Hold your finish (freeze) and notice where your lead arm finishes relative to the leg nearer the hole.

Take your normal grip again, then put your trailing hand in your pocket and stroke the same putt at the same speed. Notice how far your lead arm swings past your front leg. If your normal stroke is shorter than your lead-arm-only stroke, it means your trailing hand and wrists added power to make up the difference.

#19 Measure if you have a problem: One 10-Minute Session can determine if you have a trailing-hand power problem. If your lead-arm-only follow-through is more than two inches longer (farther past your leading leg) than your normal two-handed stroke, use the Dead-Hands Clamp (page 81) or switch to a longer shafted putting style.

Putt with a Dead-Hands Pendulum

With a conventional length putter, Perfy® (who cannot hinge his elbow or wrist joints) demonstrates the simplest putting stroke, a perfect pendulum motion.

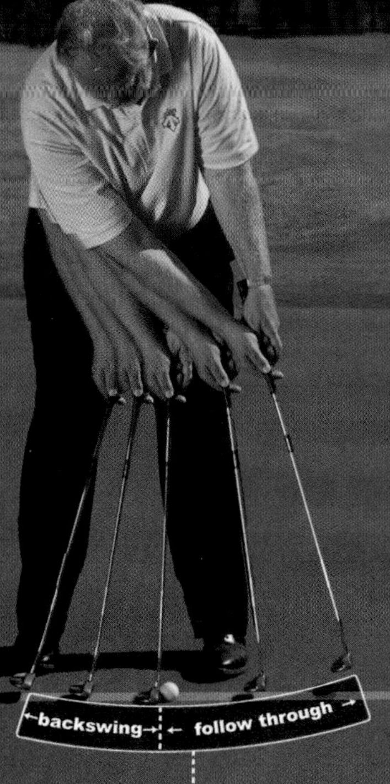

Your follow-through should be 10 to 20% longer than your back swing to provide stability through impact in a non-wrist-hinge stroke.

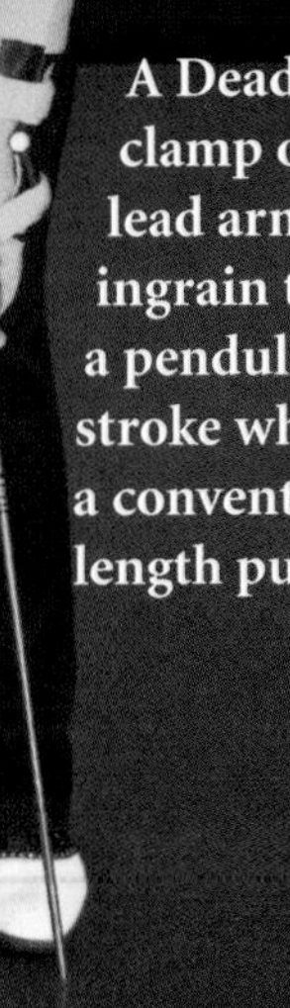

A Dead-Hands clamp on your lead arm helps ingrain the feel of a pendulum stroke when using a conventional-length putter.

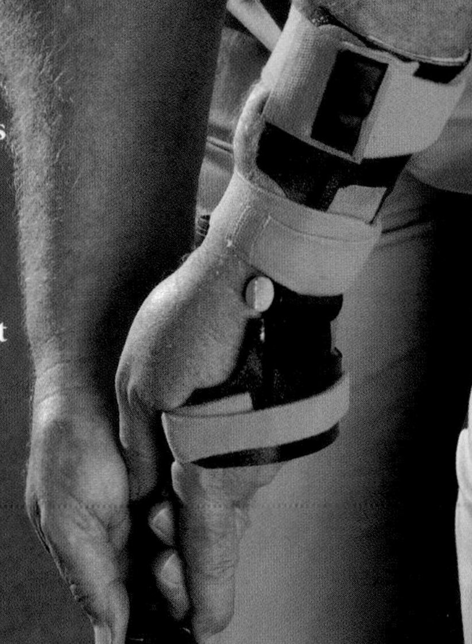

Different golfers (different body dimensions and arm/hand positions) require different clamp angles, which must be custom-fit to each player.

#20 Feel the Dead-Hands Stroke: With a conventional-length putter, six balls, a pillow, a soda can, a metronome and a Dead-Hands Clamp, you can ingrain the feel of a pure pendulum stroke. A "Dead-Hands" Session consists of putting into a pillow toward a target set behind it, with a metronome ticking at your body rhythm (page 65). Putt for five minutes with and without the clamp. As long as you feel the difference, continue repeating this drill once a week until it feels comfortable in both conditions. Putt to a different target distance each session, to get the pendulum feel for different length putts.

Test Other Putting Styles

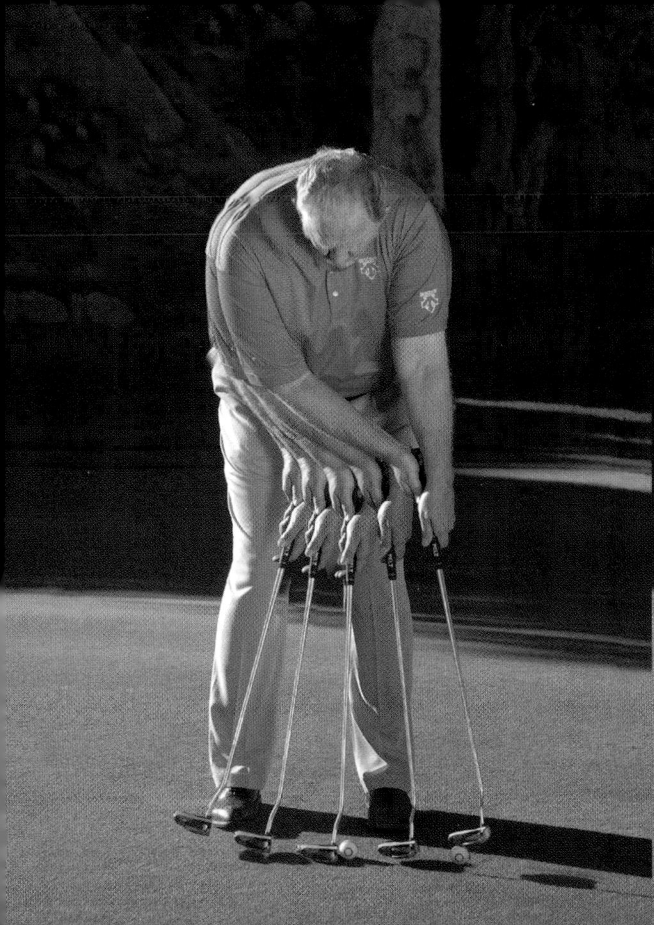

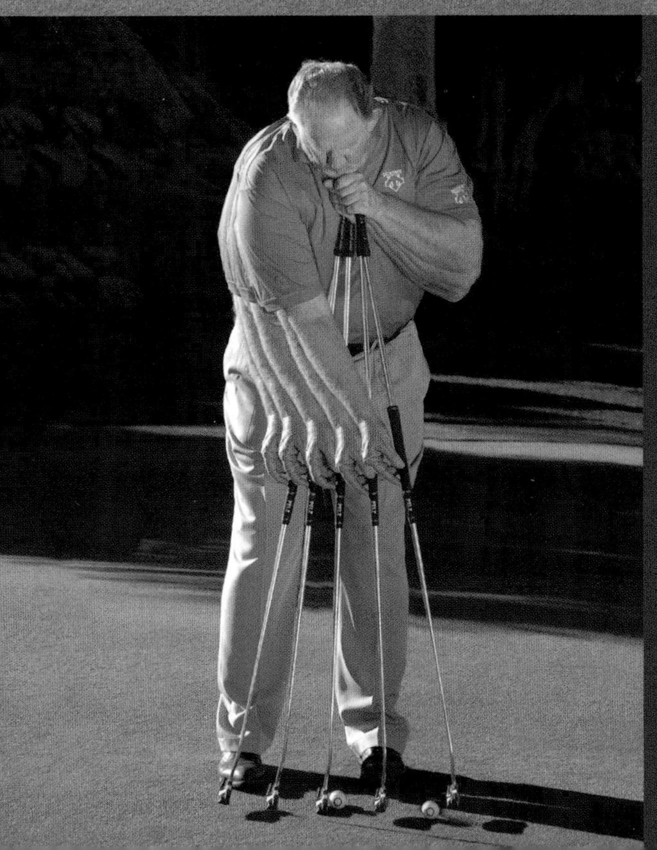

Lead-hand-low (top left), body style (top right), and long-putter strokes (lower left) can be made in perfect pendulum motions without using the small muscles of the hands and wrists. The advantage of pendulum putting is its simplicity, which promotes a consistent face angle at impact and better putting touch for speed and distance.

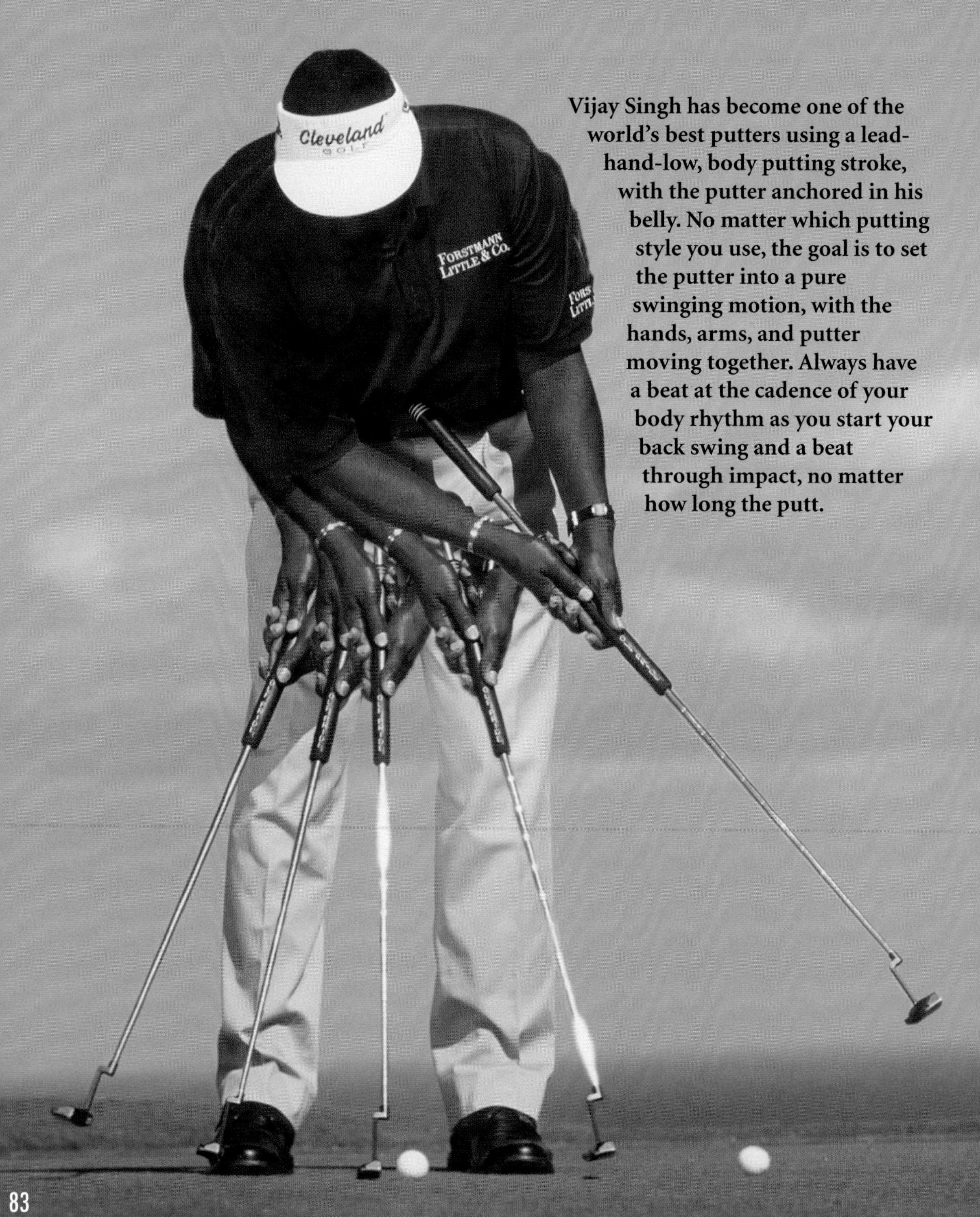

Vijay Singh has become one of the world's best putters using a lead-hand-low, body putting stroke, with the putter anchored in his belly. No matter which putting style you use, the goal is to set the putter into a pure swinging motion, with the hands, arms, and putter moving together. Always have a beat at the cadence of your body rhythm as you start your back swing and a beat through impact, no matter how long the putt.

The 3-foot stroke. A pendulum's natural rhythm depends on how long the pendulum shaft is, not on the length of its swing. This means your putter should always swing at the same rhythm back (tick) and through (tock), no matter how long the putt.

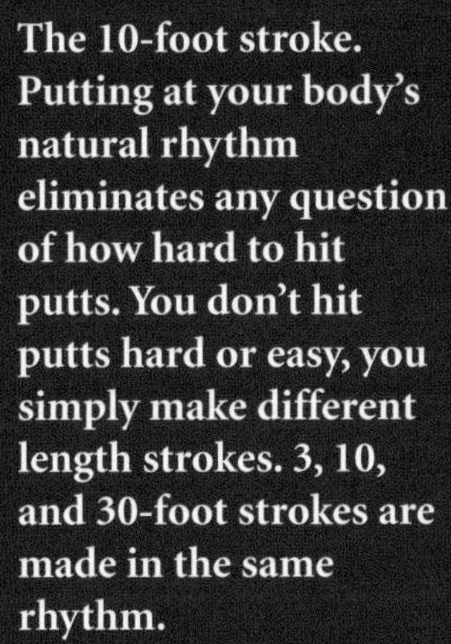

The 10-foot stroke. Putting at your body's natural rhythm eliminates any question of how hard to hit putts. You don't hit putts hard or easy, you simply make different length strokes. 3, 10, and 30-foot strokes are made in the same rhythm.

The 30-foot stroke. See how much longer it is than the 3-foot stroke? Controlling power is simple with a pendulum stroke: The length of the stroke equals the length of the putt. Long strokes for long putts, short strokes for short putts. The rhythm never varies.

#21 Test different putting styles: Test different styles against your current technique 10 minutes at a time. Mark 10 putts from 3 to 30 feet on a practice green with tees, and putt all 10 with your current technique. Then putt each putt again twice with a new (perhaps body putting) technique. Finish the test by putting all 10 again with your current putter. Keep track of how many putts you hole in each cycle so there is a winner and loser each time. Repeat the test on different days, reversing which putter goes first and last vs. the middle two cycles (putt ABBA one test, then putt BAAB the next). After several tests, you'll begin to see which method is best for you, and start putting that way on the course.

Develop a Stable Platform

I see lots of reverse-pivots (above left) when golfers first use a pendulum stroke. They think that their head sits on their shoulders, so it should rock away from the putter during the stroke. However, your head sits on your spine, not your shoulders. Your shoulders can rock without moving your head when your arms and putter swing (above right).

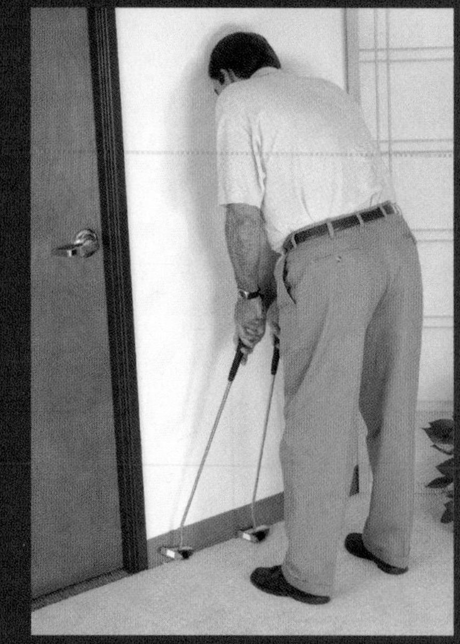

To learn if you putt with head motion, get close enough to a wall that your hair can give you feedback. Don't lean against the wall or let it hold your head.

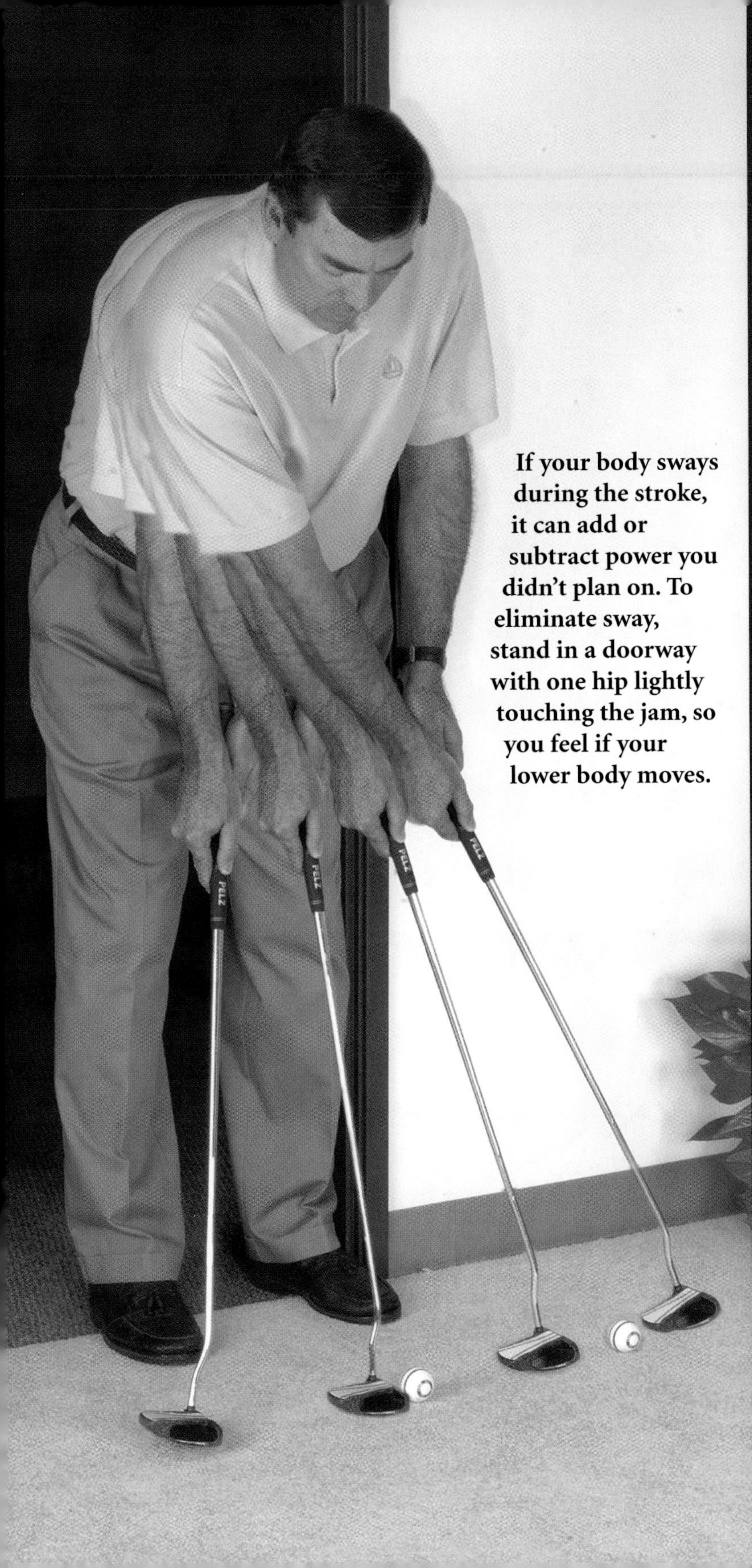

If your body sways during the stroke, it can add or subtract power you didn't plan on. To eliminate sway, stand in a doorway with one hip lightly touching the jam, so you feel if your lower body moves.

#22 Feel the solid putting base: Execute the hair-against-wall drill, then the door-jam drill, for one minute each, five times. You'll get a great 10-Minute Session of learning the feel of a pure pendulum stroke, swinging from a solid platform. Repeat this session once a week until both drills feel natural. Once you own a pendulum stroke, monthly is often enough to keep bad habits from creeping back in.

Face Angle

I've said before, and I say again: Putting success does not depend upon how much you practice but on how your putter moves through impact. And that depends upon how carefully, how smart, and how well you groove your stroke. (The state of the greens has a bit to do with it, as well.) If you learn to consistently square your putter face to the Aimline at impact, your putts will consistently start on the intended line. Then, your putting challenge will be reduced to reading greens and rolling putts at or near the optimum speed.

The direction the putter aims (face angle) at the moment of impact is the prime determinant of the line putts start on. So getting your putter face square is more important than a good putter path. Yet golfers spend most of their putting practice time working on stroke path–following through to the hole. They seldom wonder if the putter face is square or not.

It is almost impossible to be a good putter if you strike putts with a bad or inconsistent face angle. Don't neglect grooving a square face angle at impact.

Learn the Feel of Square

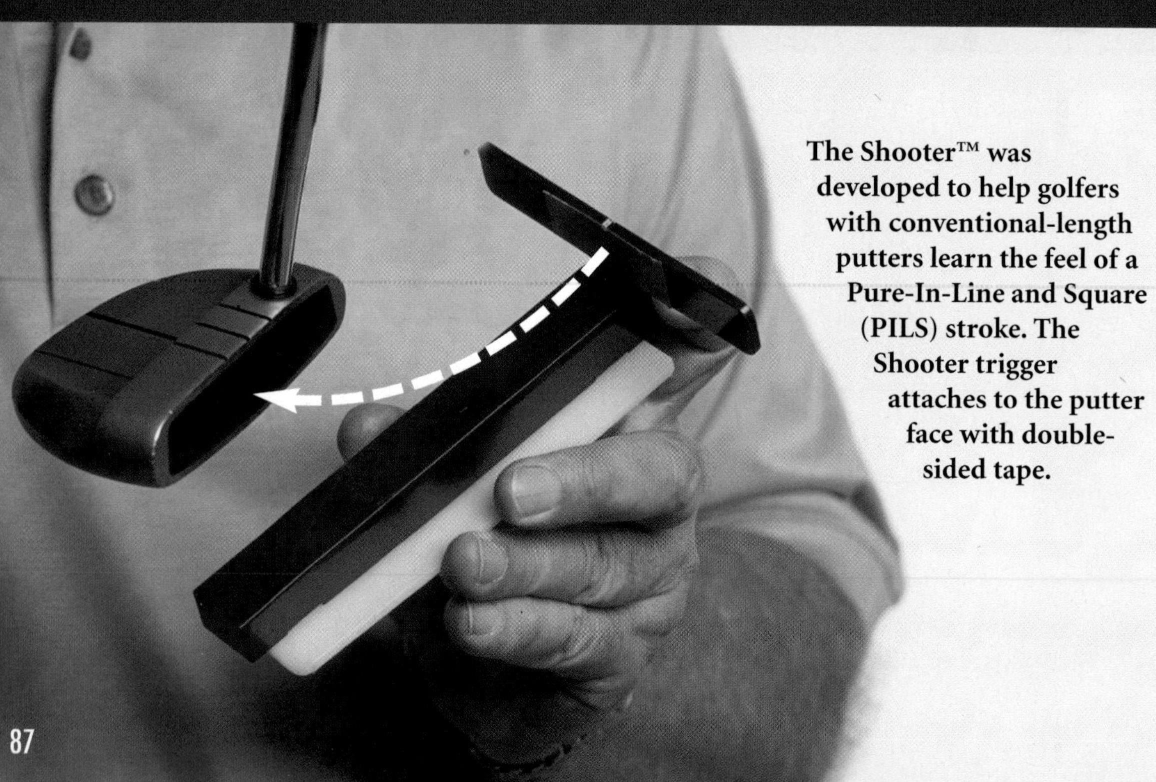

The Shooter™ was developed to help golfers with conventional-length putters learn the feel of a Pure-In-Line and Square (PILS) stroke. The Shooter trigger attaches to the putter face with double-sided tape.

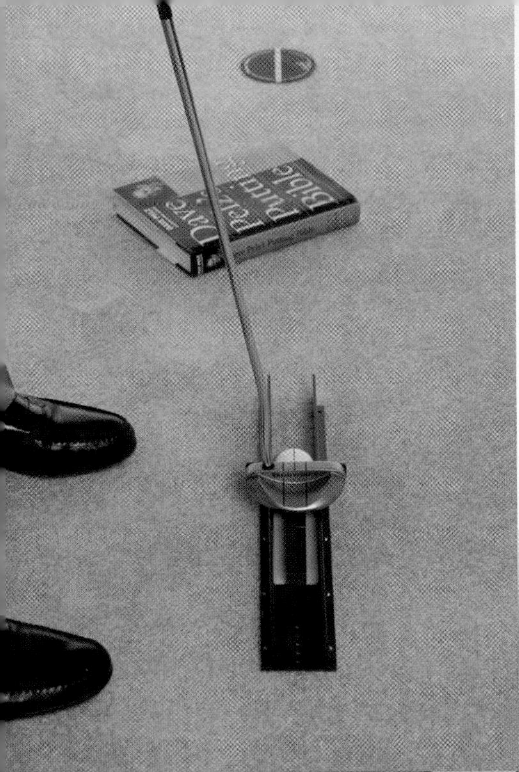

The Shooter keeps your putter in-line and square through the impact zone (can be used indoors or out). Its Teflon guide rides below the putter in the channel, to keep the putter face absolutely square.

#23 Feel square in the Shooter: Grip down an inch on your putter so with the trigger in the Shooter channel, your address position is normal. Your putter will remain above the ball and feel extra heavy, but forget that. Align the Shooter to a hole less than 6 feet away, and putt 30 balls–15 each with eyes open and eyes closed. Closing your eyes removes visual distractions and enhances your ability to feel your putter face staying square. Execute your ritual and normal pendulum stroke as best you can. The better your stroke becomes, the less pressure you'll feel from the Shooter, and the more squarely your putter will strike putts on the course.

Learn to Recognize Square Impact

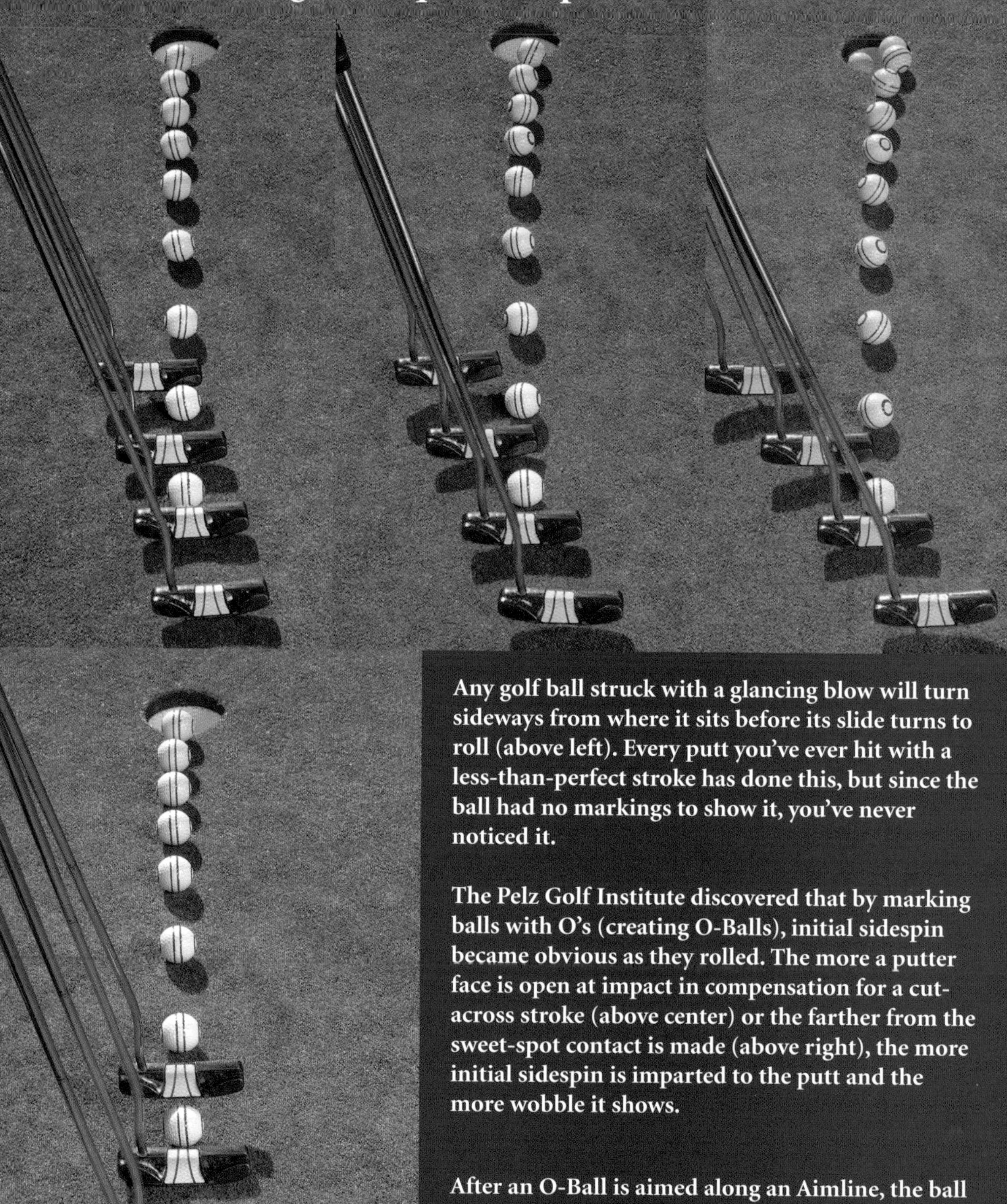

Any golf ball struck with a glancing blow will turn sideways from where it sits before its slide turns to roll (above left). Every putt you've ever hit with a less-than-perfect stroke has done this, but since the ball had no markings to show it, you've never noticed it.

The Pelz Golf Institute discovered that by marking balls with O's (creating O-Balls), initial sidespin became obvious as they rolled. The more a putter face is open at impact in compensation for a cut-across stroke (above center) or the farther from the sweet-spot contact is made (above right), the more initial sidespin is imparted to the putt and the more wobble it shows.

After an O-Ball is aimed along an Aimline, the ball can start on that line and roll wobble-free only if no initial sidespin is imparted (left). This can only happen when a square putter face moves on-line through impact and the ball solidly contacts the sweet-spot.

#24 Learn to interpret what the O-Ball tells you: This is a one-time-only session. Putt short putts (all under 5-feet) with O-Balls for 10 minutes. Focus your attention on each ball's roll. Alternate between making good strokes (putter face square and on-line) and bad strokes. For bad strokes, make cut-across strokes, inside-to-out strokes, open-face, closed-face, toe- and heel-impact strokes. Make medium-bad and really-bad strokes. The intent is to learn to recognize what O-Balls tell you about your stroke. Once you understand O-Ball feedback, it will help in both future practice and play to internalize and groove the feel of perfect strokes. Note: O-Ball feedback works for any putting style or putter length.

Groove Square at Impact

Truthboard putting has been a favorite of PGA Tour professionals for years. The Truthboard simulates a perfectly smooth, dead-straight, 3-footer. Leveling the Truthboard side-to-side (see level vial and adjustment knob) creates putts with zero break left or right. The carpet surface has no footprints (or normal green imperfections) to deflect putts, and the hole can be narrowed from standard to pro or super-pro width for advanced learners. A mirror behind the ball checks for perfect eye position.

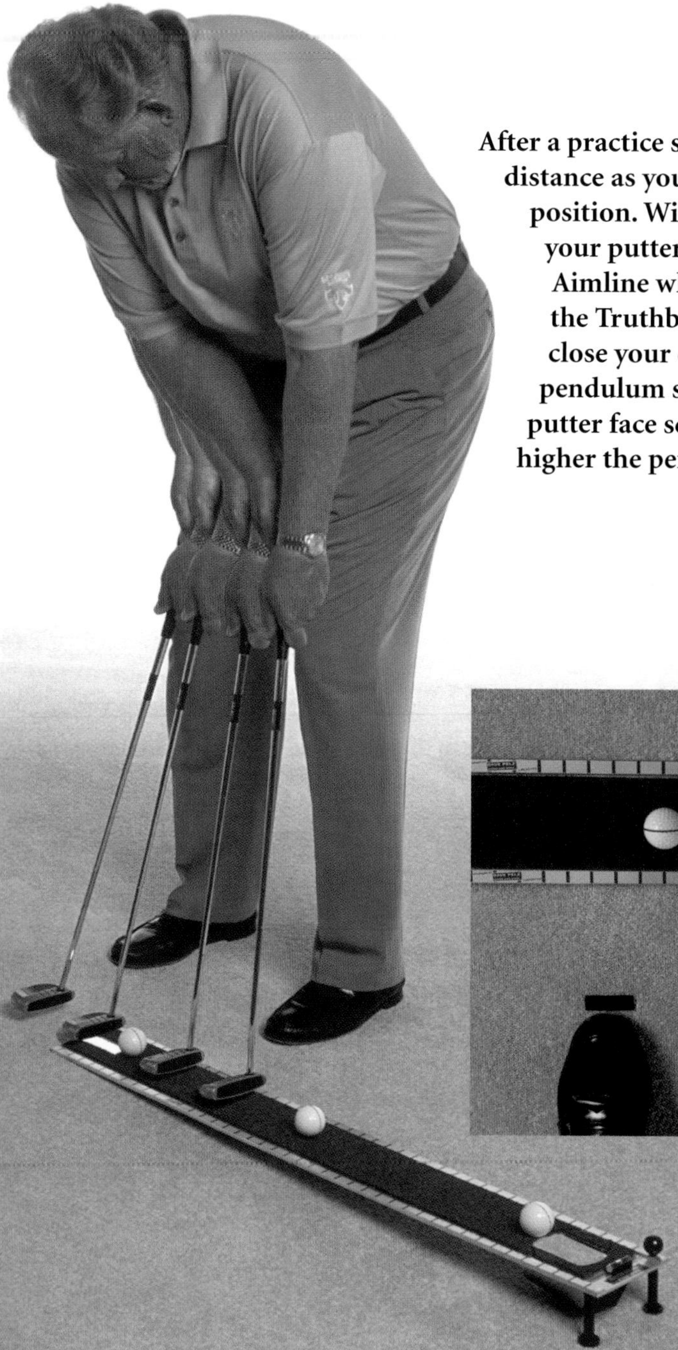

After a practice stroke, check your toe-to-ball distance as you move into your address position. With your eyes over the mirror, your putter face will be square to your Aimline when it is parallel to the lines on the Truthboard. After a perfect set-up, close your eyes and execute a dead-hands pendulum stroke. The better you feel your putter face square through impact, the higher the percentage of putts you'll make.

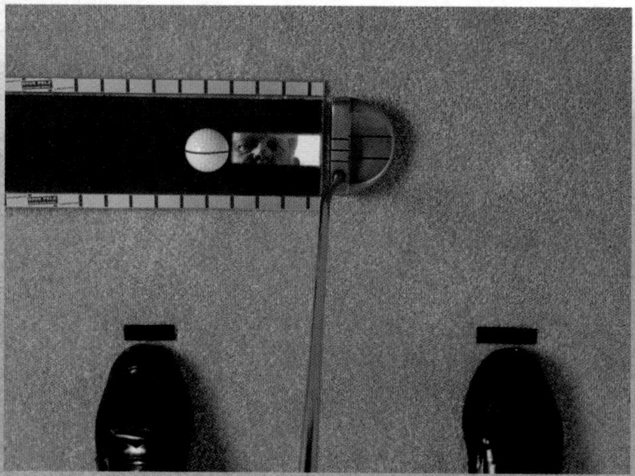

#25 Take the fear out of 3-footers: Truthboard putting is good for any putting style or putter length. For a good learning session, stroke 40 putts, closing your eyes for every other putt. When you consistently make better than 80%, shrink the hole with the next tighter hole-width magnets. Executing this session several times a week has helped many golfers conquer their fear of short putts.

In Pursuit of the Ultimate Square Putter Face

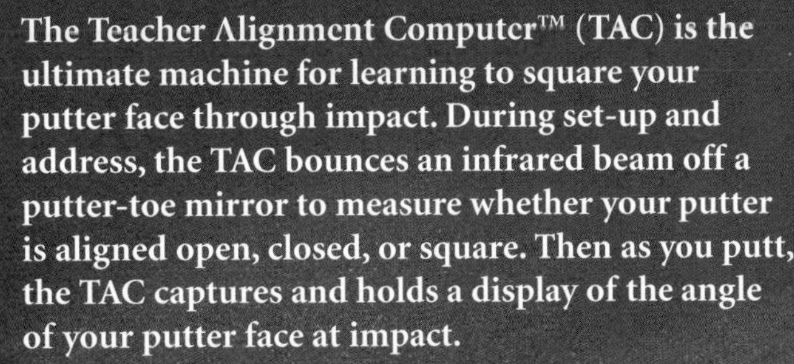

The Teacher Alignment Computer™ (TAC) is the ultimate machine for learning to square your putter face through impact. During set-up and address, the TAC bounces an infrared beam off a putter-toe mirror to measure whether your putter is aligned open, closed, or square. Then as you putt, the TAC captures and holds a display of the angle of your putter face at impact.

The central row of three green lights on top of the box signals "perfectly square." Lights to the right mean an open putter face (for right handers), while left lights indicate a closed face.

#26 Internalize the feel of square through impact: The purpose of this session is to groove your stroke so it is square through impact. In each 10-Minute Session, stroke about 30 putts in front of the TAC, to gradually improve your ability. Three accuracy settings on the TAC (standard, pro, and super-pro) will continuously challenge you as you improve (even PGA Tour pros have difficulty consistently lighting up 3 greens on the highest accuracy setting). To keep your Aimline or target consistent, use a blocking book to deflect the balls. Note: TAC sessions are good for any putting style or putter length.

Solid Impact

First the facts:
1) How fast putts roll affects how much they break.
2) The closer putts roll to the optimum speed for the break played, the more go in the hole.
3) How fast putts roll depends on how fast your putter swings and what percentage of energy is transferred to the ball at impact.
4) The closer you strike putts to the sweet-spot, the higher percentage of energy is transferred to the ball.
5) The more consistent your contact, the more consistent your speed control if your pattern is centered on the sweet-spot.

What this list means is that solid impact is vital to good putting, and golfers with good speed control are almost always good putters. It's also true that most 3-putts are the result of bad speed on the first putt. So the tighter your impact-pattern around the sweet-spot, the better your putting touch and feel will be, the rarer your 3-putts, and the more you'll make.

Making solid contact on the sweet-spot is the essence of good putting. To improve, first determine your current impact pattern. If it's good (small and sweet-spot centered), keep grooving it. If it's bad (large, and/or far from the sweet-spot), re-groove it to your putter's sweet-spot. Because even if you make otherwise perfect strokes, if they don't produce solid contact, they will leave putts short and below the hole.

Measure Your Impact Pattern

Putting with Teacher® Impact Tape on your putter face will produce dimple marks from each ball contact.

Impact patterns from three different golfers: A scratch (0) handicap player who putts very well, a 15-handicap (not a bad putter) who rarely holes anything longer than 10-feet, and a typical 30-handicapper. Some golfers never seem to contact the ball in the same place twice.

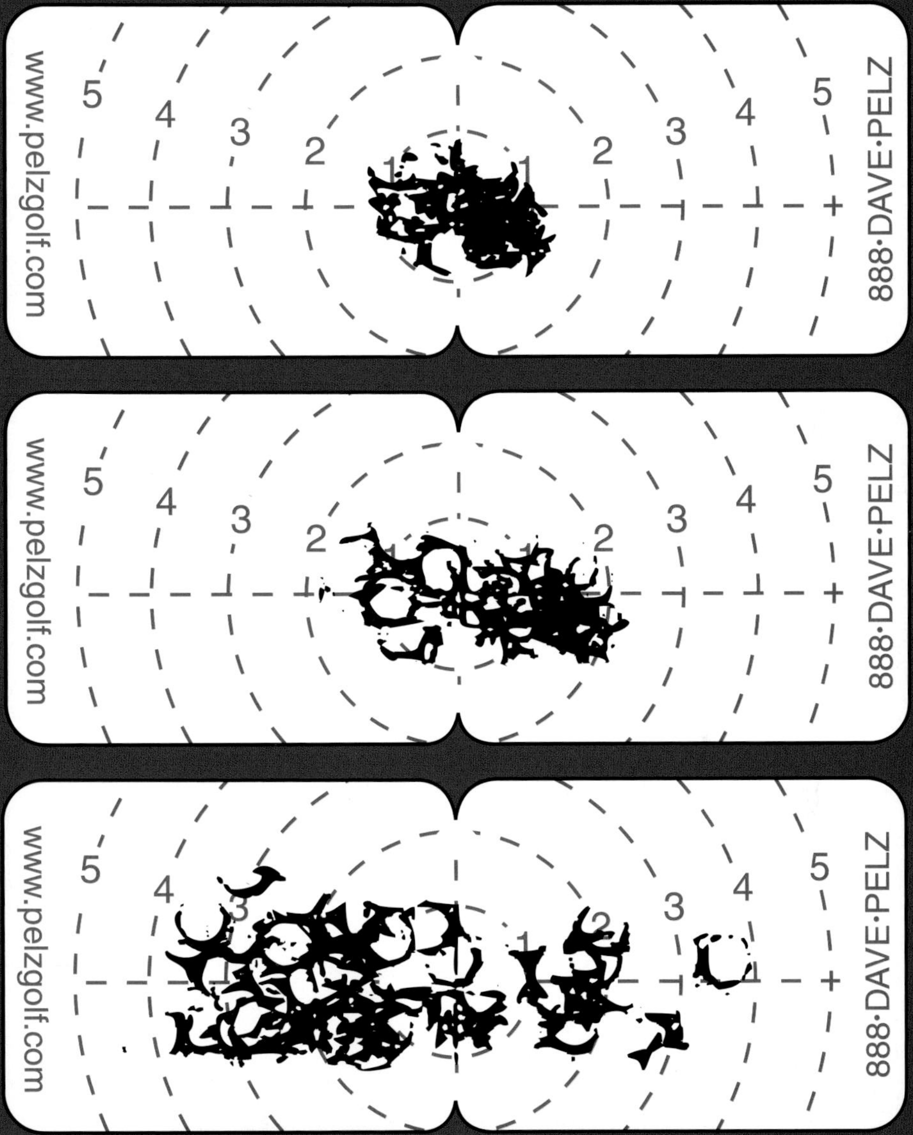

#27 Learn how consistently you transfer energy: Roll 10 putts from each of 3, 10, and 30 feet with Teacher tape on the putter face. The pattern of marks will give you a clear picture of your current impact consistency. As your pattern improves (in sessions detailed later), repeat this measurement for continuing progress reports.

Impact patterns from students in our Scoring Game Schools show a clear relationship to their handicap (above each pattern). Look at these patterns carefully.

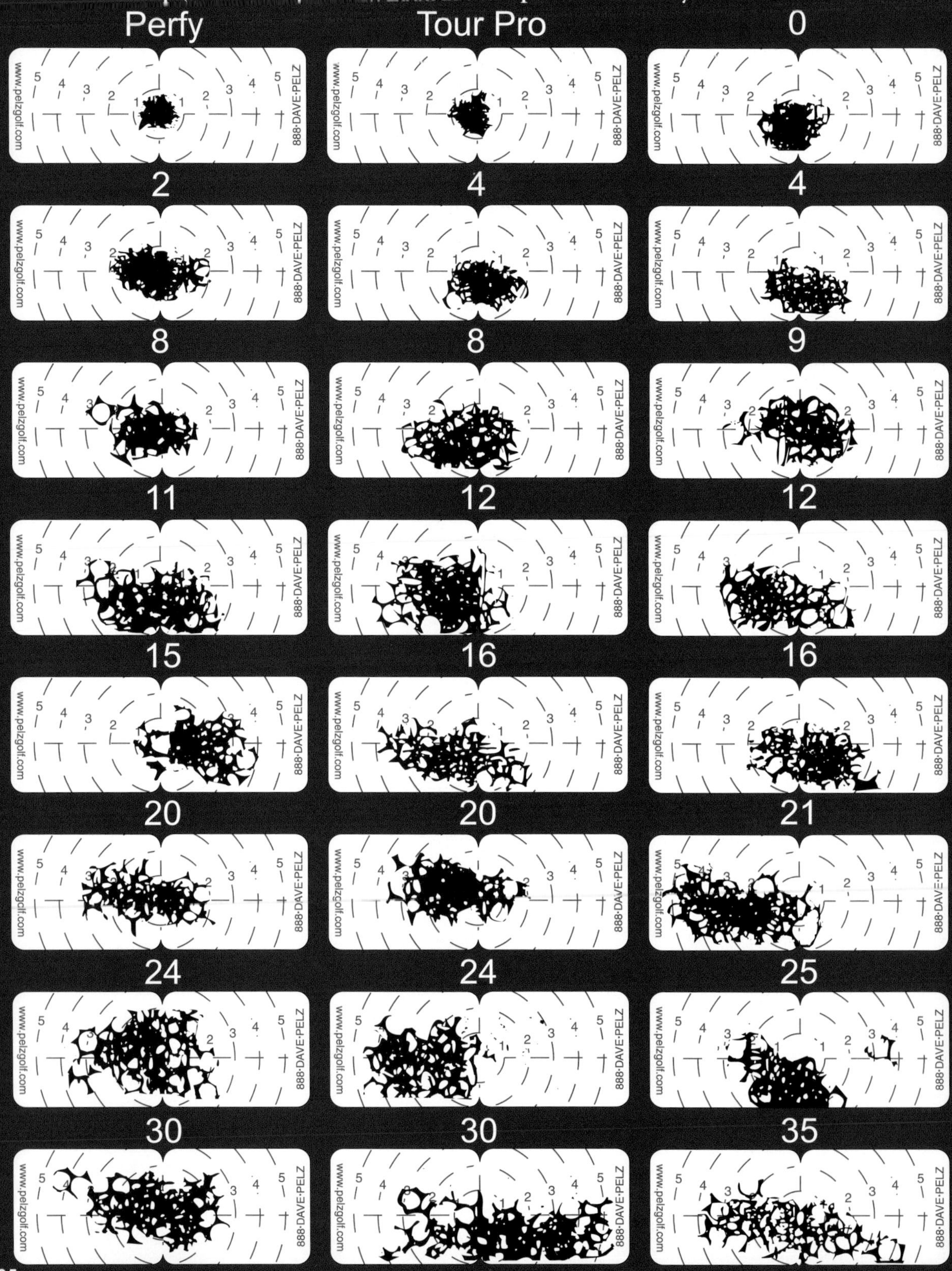

If you digest what they tell you, you'll realize that the more solidly you strike putts, the lower you'll score.

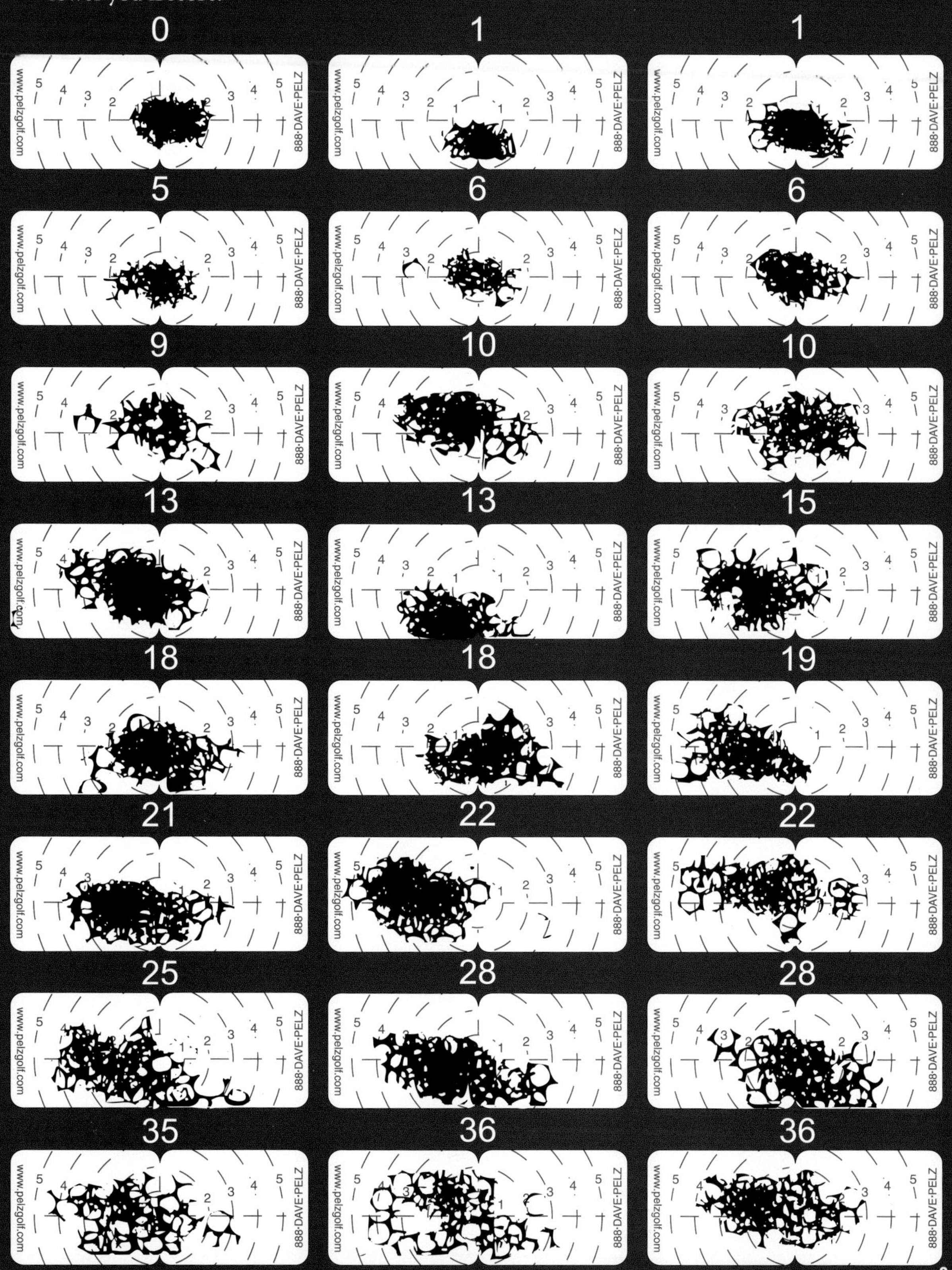

Train to the Sweet Spot

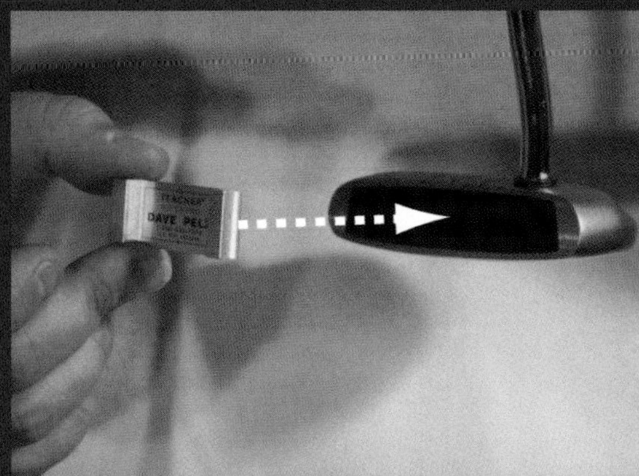

Teacher Clips stick to the putter face with double-faced tape, and have helped many PGA and LPGA Tour professionals learn to putt better. Teacher Clips come in three tolerances (standard, pro, and super pro), giving putts progressively less room to miss the sweet-spot before being "pronged."

Don't worry where balls roll when first starting to work with a Teacher Clip. Keep pillows off to each side, so you don't have to chase balls all over. Never guide your putter. Don't try to beat or fool the system. Make your normal preview stroke, step in, execute your ritual, and putt.

As you strike putts solidly (between the prongs), you'll internalize the feel of a good stroke. Toe-impact putts (for right-handed golfers) shoot severely to the left. Heel putts go right. This feedback can be quite maddening, but don't be discouraged. Every time you make solid contact, the feel of a good, solid, speed-controlled stroke goes into your memory bank.

#28 Learn to make sweet-spot strokes: As you make more solid strokes with Teacher Clips, your stroke will become grooved for solid contact, and your on-course putting will improve. A 10-Minute Teacher Clip Learning Session should produce about 20 to 25 "solid" memories. Note: Teacher Clips work for all length putters; if you consistently prong more than 50%, switch to a clip with a more generous tolerance; if pronging less than 20%, switch to a tighter clip.

Choose Your Shaft Connection (Putter Rotation Axis)

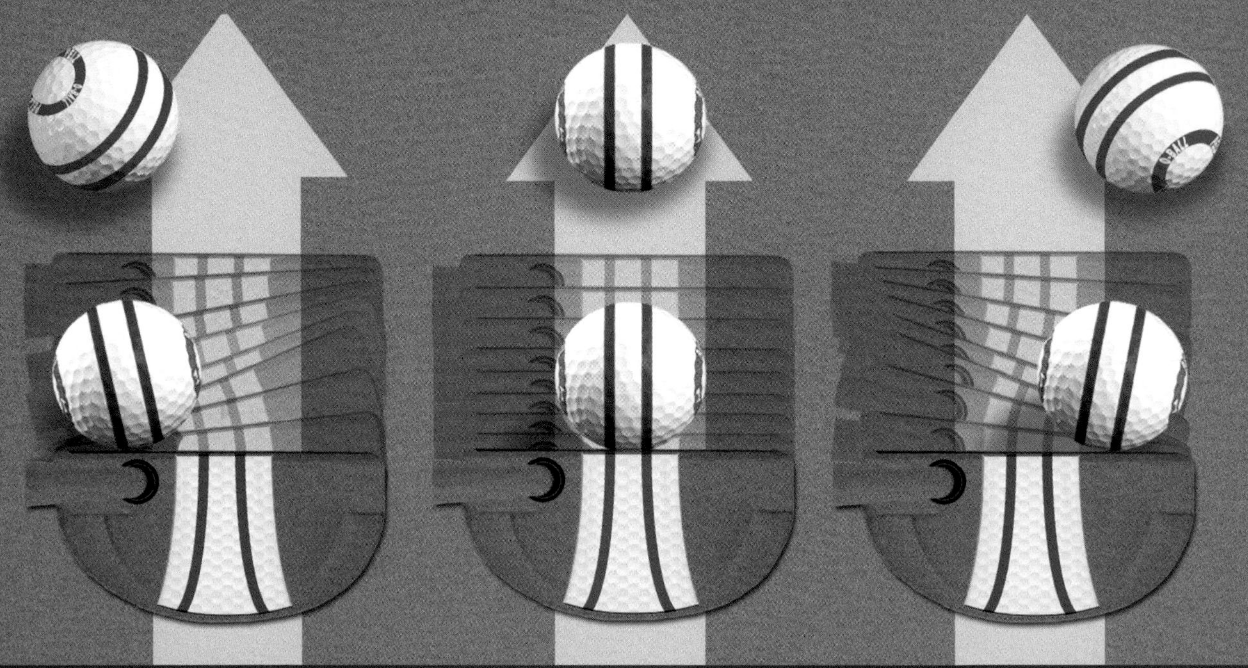

Heel impact kicks the putter toe forward, closes the face angle, and starts putts slightly left with less energy than desired (left). These putts often miss short and left.

Maximum energy transfers when the ball is struck solidly on the sweet-spot (center). The putter slows down, the ball speeds up, and both stay on line. If the Aimline and stroke speed are also good, these putts have a strong chance of finding the hole.

Toe impact kicks the putter heel forward, opens the face angle, and starts putts slightly right, with less than desired energy (right). These putts often miss short and right.

Weight distribution and shaft axis (projected through the putter head) determine how putters react to miss-hits.

Golfers tending to make impact on the heel will putt better with heel-shafted models. When contact is made between the sweet-spot and the axis of shaft rotation, the putter is less likely to close.

Golfers who tend to make impact toward the toe should use center- (or near-center) shafted putters, which keeps the rotation axis near impact and minimizes putter head turning.

#29 Fit your putter shaft to your impact pattern: Visit your golf professional and putt with several models with shaft connections correct for your impact pattern. Putt carefully, use your best strokes, and close your eyes to maximize focus on the feel of impact. Take the ones that feel best and try aiming them on a few short putts. The best putter for you is the one that feels good on most impacts, and is easy to aim, too.

Path

The direction your putter is traveling (path) when it strikes a ball affects the putt starting line less than the angle of the face. This doesn't mean that you shouldn't develop a great stroke path. Pelz Golf Institute testing shows that golfers who cut across the ball consistently open the putter face in compensation. This makes sense, because if they didn't open the face, they would consistently miss to the left. Once again, bad paths cause bad face angle corrections, and vice-versa.

Research also shows that such compensations are made subconsciously, so when golfers correct their cut-stroke paths, they continue to miss right for some time because the open-face compensations still linger. If your stroke path needs work, expect to have corresponding compensations, which also will need to be dealt with before your putting can really improve. That's how putting works–errors and their compensations must be fixed in sets.

What Your Path Is, and Should Be

The most popular path is the cut stroke, the putter traveling from outside, across the Aimline, to inside. When the putter face is opened just the right amount at impact, the ball can still roll straight. Path-left, face angle-right, ball rolling straight–this is the compensation battle many golfers fight, with consistently inconsistent results.

It has always been difficult for golfers to see or know what they are really doing right or wrong in their strokes. With an Elevated Aimline® to establish the perfect ball-hole line (on a straight putt) and an O-Ball to supply feedback on any sidespin imparted by the stroke, both path and the face angle will become obvious on video.

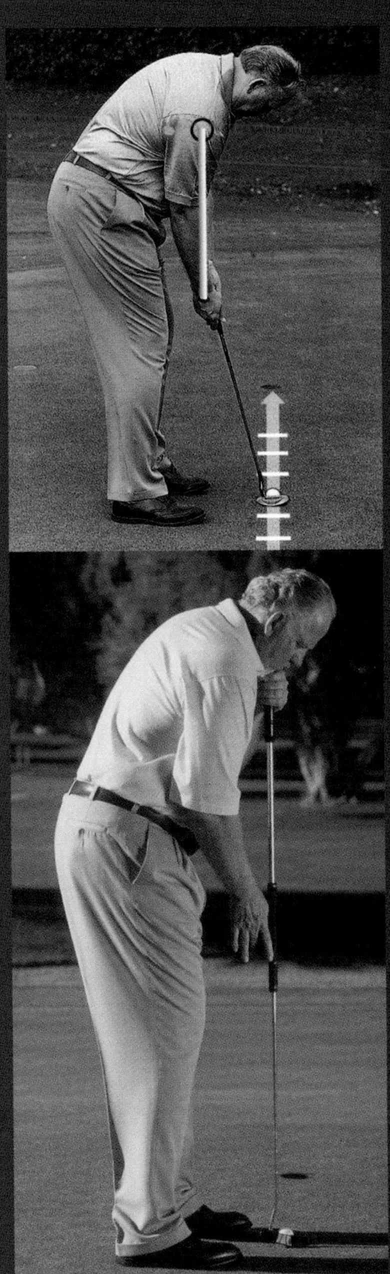

To truly know your path, measure it. What it should be depends on the putting style you use. When the plane of the stroke swing is vertical (conventional-length putter, golfer's hands under shoulders), the putter head path should be Pure In-Line and Square (PILS, or straight back and straight through, as shown above left).

For a body putter (above right), the path should move in an arc from inside to square and back to inside the Aimline, with the radius of the arc depending on how far the fixed end of the shaft is inside the line (the farther inside, the more inside the arc comes).

The path of the long putter (left) is much the same as the body putter (inside to inside), except it should not arc inside as far because the shaft is more vertical.

#30 Measure your path: Set your camcorder and tripod to look down the line over an Elevated Aimline, on a dead-straight putt. Use O-Balls to provide feedback on face-angle-induced sidespin, not otherwise visible on camera. Then putt 5 balls from three different lengths (3, 9, and 15-feet), using your normal stroke. Try to make every putt (remember, the intent here is to learn about your stroke path, not to make strokes that are different than normal). When watching your video, carefully identify what kind of stroke you have and whether or not you want to change it.

Groove your Stroke Path

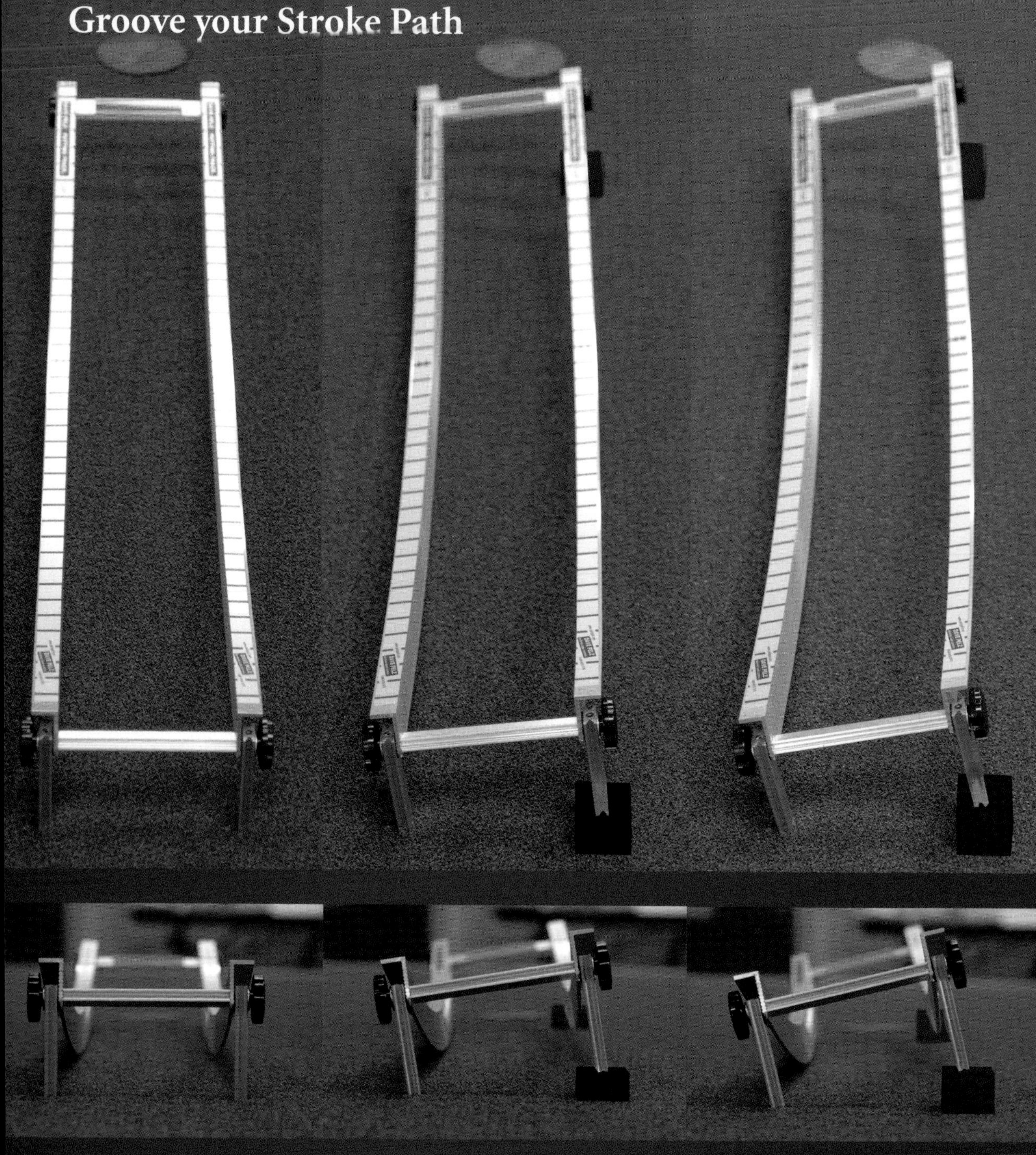

Nothing is better than the Putting Track to groove your stroke path: pure-in-line for conventional putting (left), slightly inside-to-inside for long putters (middle) and body putters (right). Track alignment to the Aimline is critical. Align the Track straight and level to the target for conventional putting. Then elevate the two outside legs by 1/2-inch and 3/4-inch respectively to create the inside-to-inside arc for long and body putting.

Here, I'm lining-up the Track for conventional putting. Notice how I look to make sure the Track is aimed perfectly. The straight part of the putter shaft runs up through the center of the Track to the intended target, or true break point on a breaking putt.

Start with a 1" clearance between your putter and Track rails.

#31 Groove your stroke path at home (or office): Set the Track rails one-inch wider than the head length of your putter, and carefully align it to your Aimline. Centered in the track, there should be a half-inch clearance on either side of the putter head before you hear the clank (feedback) from off-line strokes. Conduct this session indoors, and always make a preview stroke before stepping in to putt. Don't worry about where the ball goes. Do care about making pure, non-clanking strokes in the Track. To use the Track for body or long putters, aim it straight along the Aimline when level, then, without moving the inside legs, raise the outside two legs. Putt for 10 minutes each session, until you can make 80% of your strokes (about 20 out of 25) without any noise. Only then do you reduce the Track rail tolerance in future sessions.

Take your Path to the Course

The Easy Roller™ is for use only with conventional-length putters. It sticks on the putter face with double-sided tape and captures the ball at address. The Easy Roller's function is to drag the ball back and through with your stroke, releasing the ball in the direction of your follow-through.

The Easy Roller releases the putt about 6 inches after impact. If your putter path is heading substantially left by that time, the putt also will roll left (left). Putting short putts with the Easy Roller will help you learn a good feel for following through along the Aimline (right).

Once your stroke is grooved to stay on-line for straight putts, you should try the same stroke on breaking putts. Easy Roller putting will help you feel comfortable following through along your Aimline, even when the putt breaks substantially.

#32 Groove your follow-through: You may have been told to always follow-through to the hole. That advice is for dead-straight putts only. Learn a follow-through that travels down your Aimline and path will never be a problem. You should be able to make more short putts with the Easy Roller than without it, because it eliminates face angle and impact errors from your stroke. It will take several minutes of putting in the first session to get used to the ball moving with your putter on the backstroke, but don't let this put you off. In a 10-Minute Easy Roller Session, you should be able to hole at least 30 putts from inside 6 feet.

10 minute

⑤ Optimize Artistic Skills

In art, there is more to seeing than meets the eye. In golf, there is more to putting than stroke mechanics.

In putting, if you don't have knowledge of the conditions of the green surface, your mind can't comprehend how long putts will play, and you don't know what to expect after your ball starts rolling. This means you don't have good "touch". A golfer with poor touch doesn't know what needs to be done to roll the ball to the hole.

If on the other hand a golfer has good touch, knows precisely the energy required to roll a

ball 17 inches past a hole, but doesn't know how to supply that energy to the putt, he has a poor "feel" for putting speed and distance.

Touch and feel are related, but they do not come in the same package. While some golfers have both good touch and feel and some have neither, many golfers have one good and the other bad. More importantly, having both good touch and feel won't make you a good putter if you also don't have a good putting stroke. Just as true, superb putting stroke mechanics don't by themselves guarantee good putting if the golfer doesn't have good touch and feel.

Ball Sports Take Getting Used To

I grew up with a ball in my hand, be it a basketball, baseball, football, beach ball, volleyball, marble, or golf ball. Many men have done this. The same is not true for most women however. My daughters certainly didn't spend their youths on the baseball diamond or football field.

Not growing up with sports such as these has left its mark on many women, who as a group generally putt worse than men. It has nothing to do with talent or even stroke mechanics. Missing out on a childhood of ball games means their touch and feel are less accurately developed. On the flip side of their pre-conditioning, women in our schools seem to learn and improve faster. This may be due to their open-minded, insightful, and visually oriented approach...key elements of better putting,

Putting touch and feel are learned skills, not learned from a book or video, but by reading greens, stroking and watching how putts roll. Learning good putting touch and feel is cerebral (in the mind's eye) and almost entirely experiential. They cannot be accurately developed however, without consistent putting stroke mechanics. Assuming you learned how to deal with those in chapter 4, it's now time to talk about your touch, feel, and rhythm.

Nothing Rolls Like a Ball

I'll never forget the day Jack Lemmon, Peter Jacobsen, and I (as Lemm's caddy) had a real chance to make the cut in the AT&T Pebble Beach National Pro-Am. Lemm got so petrified and put so much pressure on himself to perform that he couldn't get his putts to the hole. He was so nervous, he left putts short from 3, 5, and 2 feet on consecutive holes.

Our playing companion and friend Fulton Allem walked over and whispered to Lemm, "Remember, nothing rolls like a ball." It helped. Amazingly, just that thought helped. Lemm started thinking about something other than the tournament, visualizing rolling balls over various surfaces. He putted well from then on (although we still missed the cut, but by only two shots) as he smiled and visualized how easily balls will roll if you give them a little starting speed.

If you've never watched or played "Ultimate Chaos Pool" before, it's difficult to imagine what will happen the first time you do. If you've never putted fast greens, and never seen a 25-foot putt break 25 feet on the way to the hole, then you're not likely to have good touch, or a good putting round, the first time you play in the U.S.Open.

You can even help your putting by watching other ball sports. Playing and watching pool is good for putting touch. Similarly, if you've seen golf balls roll on concrete and sand (with extremely different results), it might help you imagine how putts will behave on U.S.Open or dew-covered greens, early in the morning.

Time erodes (but does not destroy) Touch and Feel

Time erodes and dulls your touch and feel, making it slightly out-of-focus like this picture. Don't expect your touch or feel to be sharp if you haven't putted in a while, because your muscles forget details, and lapse into an "older-memory" state. This is the first thing that happens when golfers lay-off for a while.

Once you learn good touch and feel, you never totally lose it. The information is in your brain, never to be forgotten, just as you never forget how to ride a bicycle. The better you develop touch and feel, the easier it is to retrieve and return them to sharp focus, after a long layoff.

#33 Learn how golf balls roll: This may sound crazy, but try putting on strange surfaces. For fast surfaces, putt on flat cement roads or driveways, hall carpets in hotels, tile floors, and commercial-grade short-pile carpets. For slow surfaces, putt on the tee boxes at good golf courses, long-pile home carpeting, and in the first cut of rough on your course. Don't simply hack balls around and laugh. Try to putt balls to specific targets, experiencing how difficult it is to control speed and distance.

Race drivers push their cars too fast, and sometimes over the edge- to find the line between optimum performance and too much. Putting on strange surfaces can give you experience at the extreme ends of touch.

Touch

Touch is knowing in your mind's eye how much energy you need to supply to a putt, to roll it from point A to point B before you see it roll. Feel is knowing in your body how to supply it. If you don't have good touch, then all of the feel in the world (for making a particular stroke perfectly) won't do you any good, because you won't know which stroke to make. Learn touch first: feel after.

Having good touch is sensing, just by watching his stroke, that a playing companion stroked a putt too firmly (or too weakly) before you see the ball roll.
Having bad touch is putting just as you intended, contacting the ball solidly on the sweet-spot, thinking "aaahhhh, the perfect stroke," then looking up and seeing the ball roll 12 feet past the hole.

Establish a Metric

An easy metric (method of measuring distance) is the 3-foot stride. Mark 3-foot intervals at home, then walk back and forth along them, adjusting your stride to match: 3 feet per step. Once you've learned a 3-foot stride, you can accurately walk off distances on the greens. It's always better to know the length of a putt than to guess how long it is based on how long it appears.

Learn Reference Putts

I have set up three reference putts with Phony Holes (thin rubber discs which look like holes and serve as targets) at 40 and 50 ft, and the flagstick at 60 ft. When your touch gets good at these distances, everything around them will be good also. A year from now, you should "own" these reference distances. Any time you face a 40, 50, or 60-footer on the course, your touch will tell you how much energy the putt needs.

Touch is knowing in your mind's eye how much energy it will take to roll the ball to the hole. Try bowling or tossing the ball to the hole with an underhand swing (this should be easier than striking the ball with a putter, because there is no danger of a miss-hit).

Now putt two balls to the same hole you tossed to, above. The toss told you how much energy is required. Make solid contact and you should be able to putt it about the right distance. Repeat the toss and two putts to different holes at different distances. When working on touch, don't putt more than two balls to the same distance consecutively. Keep changing distances, so your mind has to work and learn the correlation between the length of the stroke required vs. the length of the putt. This is what touch is all about.

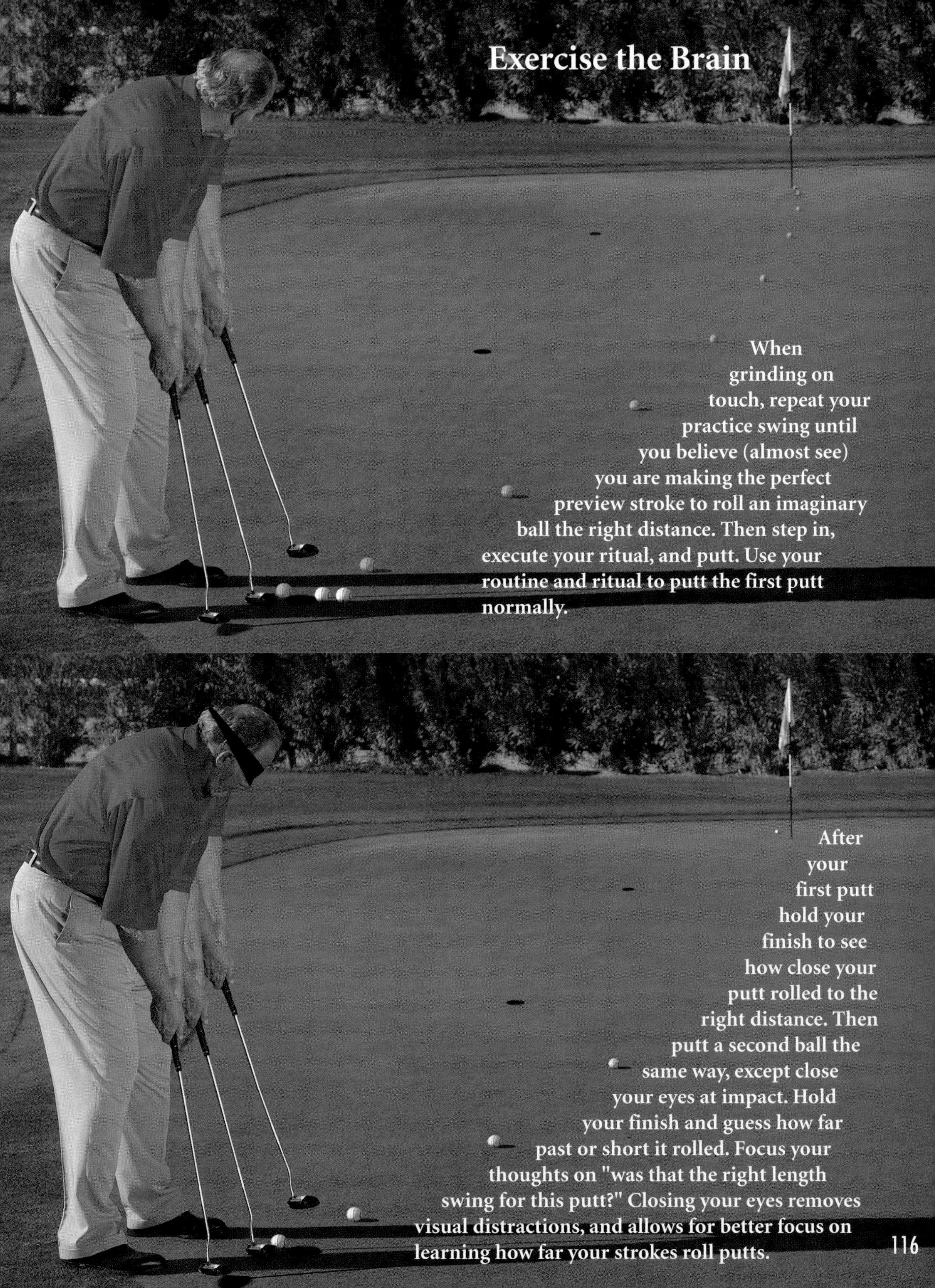

Exercise the Brain

When grinding on touch, repeat your practice swing until you believe (almost see) you are making the perfect preview stroke to roll an imaginary ball the right distance. Then step in, execute your ritual, and putt. Use your routine and ritual to putt the first putt normally.

After your first putt hold your finish to see how close your putt rolled to the right distance. Then putt a second ball the same way, except close your eyes at impact. Hold your finish and guess how far past or short it rolled. Focus your thoughts on "was that the right length swing for this putt?" Closing your eyes removes visual distractions, and allows for better focus on learning how far your strokes roll putts.

The Three Hole Triangle Drill

3 Known Distances

1
36'
29'
2
3
22'

By walking off and measuring three distances, then putting two balls in the direction of the arrows (eyes open for the first putt, closed for the second), you can practice 12 different putts of known distances.

6 Putts-Clockwise

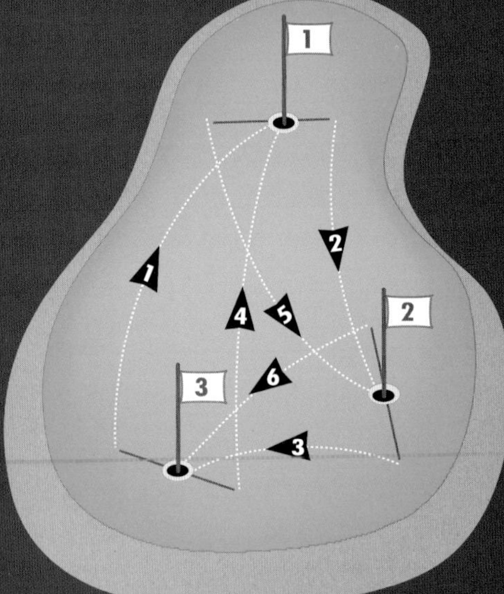

6 Putts-Counterclockwise

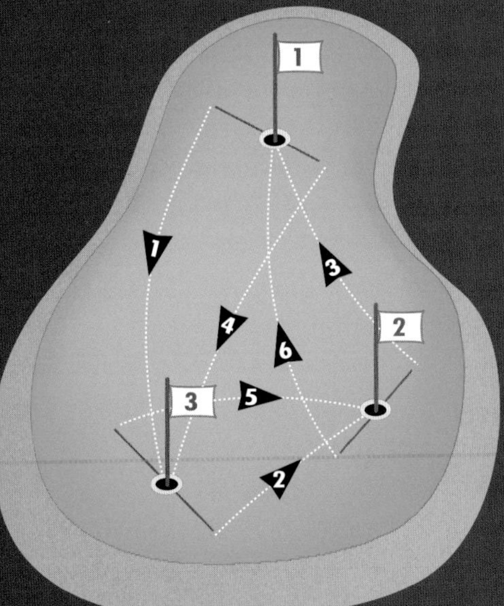

#34 Develop your Touch: Set tees in your yard at 3-foot intervals, and walk back and forth using 3-foot strides until you can close your eyes and arrive at the last marker on an even stride. In the next session, mark off putts at 40, 50, and 60 –feet on a practice green (reference putts). First bowl, then putt two balls to each distance, closing your eyes on the second putts. After you feel confident of your touch on the three reference-putt distances, try several 10-Minute Sessions on the three-hole drill, putting two balls around the triangle. Always close your eyes and guess the results of the second putt.

Feel

Feel is knowing how you need to move, and how it's going to feel to do what your touch says is required, for a putt. Feel will come and go, good one day and bad the next. Feel also can be affected by your level of concentration at the moment. And just as touch is not enough for good putting, neither is feel alone sufficient.

Once your touch "sees" a putt, your feel is required to provide it's speed and distance control. You must forget everything else (especially any desire or pressure to make it), and focus only on a feel for speed and distance. Hopefully by this time your stroke mechanics are on "automatic" control, you've read the green, and your touch has told you what to do. All that's left is to feel the stroke needed to roll the putt at optimum speed.

Set up Reference Putts

Repeated attempts with detailed feedback are the keys to learning feel. The reference putts I recommend are: 10, 20, 30, 40, 50, and 60 feet. Choose any three distances (for the day) and set up two Phony Holes and one real hole, for feel practice (use one real hole because it's always fun to see a few putts drop out of sight).

Eyes Closed for Maximum Feel

This is the set up for a 20-foot feel session, which is important, because you'll face more 20-footers than any other "first-putt" length. Sometimes it's good to have uphill and downhill putts. In some sessions set up across a slope so you work on left-to-right, and right-to-left feel. The more often you experience the perfect feel of a putt, the easier it is to recall that feel when facing that same putt on the course.

Putt three balls, always the last one with your eyes closed, to maximizc your awareness of feel. As you strike the third putt, close your eyes and guess if it rolled the perfect distance, stopped short, or rolled too far past (more than 17 inches).

#35 Fine Tune your Feel: : Putt for 10 minutes in competition, putting each ball with your eyes closed. If you can't find a companion, putt three balls each way between two holes 20 feet apart until you stop nine in a row within 34 inches (the length of your putter) past the hole. For the last ball, tell yourself that it, too, must stop within one-putter-length past the hole or go in. If not, you'll stay and do another 10-Minute Session.

Lag Putting

Research from the Pelz Golf Institute reveals that:
1) For the average golfer, more strokes can be saved on the greens by eliminating 3-putting than by improving stroke mechanics.
2) Golfers leave an increasing percentage of putts short of the hole, as putt length increases.
3) The more uphill the putt, the more likely golfers are to leave it short.
4) Even Tour pros leave most long and uphill putts short.

An obvious conclusion is that since good putting strokes sacrifice power for accuracy, they suffer on long and uphill putts. Recent testing has revealed a solution to this problem, made possible by changing putting techniques when dealing with putts that require significant power. The solution is called the "Chipputt".

Learn to Chipputt

Chipping with your putter is called "Chipputting." Just as in chipping, a slight body turn can add a little power to your swing, making it easier to get the ball to the hole. Position the ball slightly forward in your stance, stand upright, and chip with your putter. Expect to use the same size swing as if you were chipping with a 5-iron.

Most golfers find the optimum distance to "changeover" from putting to Chipputting somewhere between 50 and 100 –feet.

Golfers who struggle with their lag putting with a long or body putter, will also find Chipputting with it difficult. The solution? Consider carrying a conventional-length putter just for long or lag putts and Chipputting. Remember, avoiding 3-putts is essential to lower scores, and it is acceptable to carry two putters, if you score better doing so. Remove a long iron from your bag to make room for the second putter. I'm willing to bet you won't miss that long iron, and lag putting better *will* improve your scores.

#36 Evaluate your lag putting skills: Take six balls to a practice green and use tees to mark off every 10-feet from 50 to 100 feet from a hole. Putt six balls from each distance, three with your normal putting stroke and three Chipputting. Start at 50 feet and move out until the difference in your lag ability becomes obvious. In a good 10-Minute Session, you can find your changeover (to Chipputting) distance.

Repeat the session on different days to see if the changeover distance between your regular lag putting and Chipputting is consistent on level putts. Then try the drill on up and downhill putts. The changeover distance will be shorter on uphill putts (which require more power), and longer on downhillers. Once you're comfortable with Chipputting, use it on the course to stop 3-putting.

6 Reading Greens

Putting is a combination of science and art. It is the science of spheres, gravity, angles, slopes, energy transfer and stroke mechanics. It is the art of feel, touch, and sensing the break of putts rolling on unknown surfaces. It is also much more of course, but of these aspects of putting, the black sheep of the herd is by far green reading.

Most golfers work on stroke mechanics ad nauseam without ever thinking of improving their ability to read greens. Although everyone knows a perfect stroke is useless if you don't know where to aim it, they all love stroke mechanics and ignore green reading.

Now be honest: When was the last time you worked on improving your green reading? Have you ever? Do you know how? What have you done to improve your ability to *see* how much putts break? Have you worked on your green reading imagination lately? Well, it's time.

You Probably Under-Estimate the Break

The Pelz Golf Institute tested 1,500 golfers over a period of two years. During that time, they were asked to read a putt and tell us how much it would break. Of those 1,500 golfers–who included 50 PGA Tour professionals, every single one of them under-estimated the true break, while none estimated too-much break. Incredibly, not one out of 1,500 golfers read too much or even enough break!

The average estimate of break by these 1,500 golfers was about one-third of the true break of the putt. I mention this test because you should now assume that you've always under-read your putts. Don't feel bad or insulted. Because after years of intense study following the above-mentioned test, I have concluded that it is perfectly natural for golfers to under-read break. Here's why.

Understand Gravity

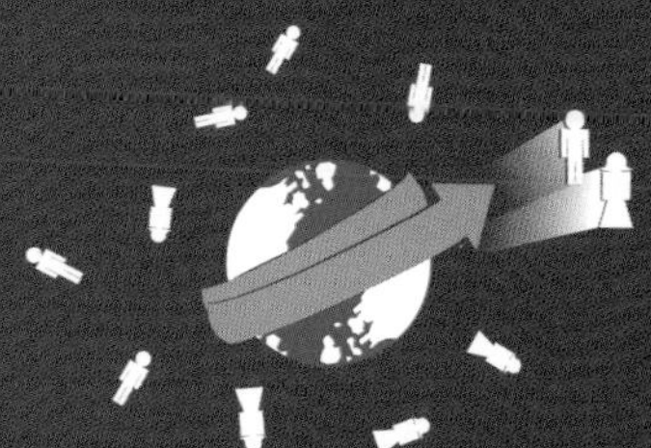

Nobody understands why the mass of the earth attracts and pulls bullets, arrows, baseballs, and your golf balls toward its center. But everybody knows that it does! Gravity exists! And we all must deal with it! (Don't complain, without gravity we all would be flung into space by the earth's spin)

The slower a body moves, the more time gravity has to act on it, pull it down, and curve its trajectory, as illustrated by the bullet, arrow and baseball below.

Gravity pulls golf balls down all the time. As putts roll, the pull of gravity causes their path to curve in the direction of a down-slope. The slower you roll a putt, the higher you must start it above the hole to have any chance of making it.

Said another way, the faster the green, the slower your putts must roll to stop near the hole, and the more they will break, for any given slope.

Estimate the Break

Drop a Phony Hole and ball on a slope to create a putt you know will break. Then read (guess) how much. Don't feel bad that you don't *know* how much it will break (nobody knows, even Tiger Woods guesses about break, and sometimes he's wrong).

Place a tee by the hole on what you think is the line on which your ball should start rolling to make the putt at perfect speed. The distance of the tee from the hole is your estimate of how much the putt will break. The line from your ball to the tee is your Aimline.

Watch the True Roller Make the Putt

Now look at what would happen if Eddie used our True Roller (a research tool we use to measure what the true break is), to roll a ball at your tee. See how it misses the hole low? After moving the True Roller two times to start balls higher, he makes the putt at perfect speed.

Mark the Aimline

After he finds where to aim the True Roller to make the putt (the Aimline), he marks it with an Elevated Aimline® (elastic thread stretched between two stakes), pointing exactly in line with the final True Roller aim.

When watching the True Roller roll putts (or any putt), the vision of where the ball rolled quickly disappears from your mind. To show you the complete ball track all at once, I've stopped balls as Eddie rolled them one after another, marking the exact ball track of each roll.

Learn the Anatomy of a Putt

Now Eddie looks from behind the starting point of the putt and *sees* the Aimline, ball track, visual break, true break, and the true break point (all marked in the photo). This is reality: the perfect ball track, started on the perfect Aimline, at the perfect speed.

I wish you could have rolled the balls yourself, but studying this photograph will have to do for now. Make sure you understand each term: ball-hole line; ball-track; visual break (the maximum distance the putt departs from the ball-hole line); true break; and true break point.

Understand the Reason for Under-reading

Now think back to when you first read this putt. You imagined a ball rolling into the hole as shown here, and assumed this is about how much break you should play (remember, this is where you put the tee).

Understand why Apex Putting doesn't Work

For your initial read to be correct, the putt would have to roll on the straight line you started it on, up to the apex (high point of its break), then curve down into the hole. This however, is not the way gravity curves putts.

It's natural to underestimate break because you only see the latter part of your putt's roll, as it breaks near the hole, and you assume (incorrectly) that's all the break there is. You never see how far it broke in the first two-thirds of its roll, because your head is down at impact and the ball moves out of view quickly.

See Reality

Imagine you've measured the true break of a putt, and installed this Elevated Aimline. Imagine looking from behind the ball, down the Aimline at the reality of where the putt must be aimed to have it roll on the optimum ball track. This is *seeing* the putt. Recognize where the Aimline is compared to that tee you put out there. Tell yourself (internalize) you must always aim above where you expect to see your putts roll, above the apex of the ball track, to get them to roll there.

ALERT! There is still a Problem...

Knowing what you now know, if you putted this putt instead of Eddie, I guarantee you'd miss it high, above the hole. Before I tell you why, please do the 10-Minute Session on the facing page.

#37 Believe in gravity: On opposite ends of a piece of paper, draw a ball and a hole. Then draw a curved path line (ball track) connecting the two, assuming an overhead view looking straight down on a 10-foot putt on a severely sloping green.

Draw the ball-hole line (straight between the ball and the hole), and draw in the visible break, which is the maximum distance between the ball track and the ball-hole line. Next, draw a line out from the hole (on the high side), which is three times as long as the visible-break line. At the end of this line make a small circle, to mark the true break point. And finally, draw the Aimline from the ball to the true break point.

Looking at your sketch, you should see that true break is about three times greater than visible break, as seen from above. Also see that if you drew one more line from the ball to the apex of the ball track, it would be about half way between the ball-hole line and the Aimline, as seen from a golfer's view from behind the ball.

Now understand: if you go to the course and start doubling the break you see from behind the ball, which is actually tripling the visible break (look at your drawing), you'll probably miss many putts high. Why? Because after years of reading putts too low (without knowing it), your stroke has developed subconscious compensations to always start your putts on a higher line. Without those compensations, you never would have come near holing any breaking putts. It will take some time of putting to a new, correct break point for those in-stroke compensations to go away. You need to re-train your sub-conscious and get rid of your in-stroke habit of compensating for an under-read break.

Experience Reality

Knowing the truth is great, but it does nothing for you if you don't train yourself to take advantage of it. Knowing you should play more break is different from actually doing it.

When you first play more break in your putts, and then miss them on the high side, it can be very confusing. You may assume you over-did it and played too much break, but that is wrong. Confused? Probably, but hang in with me. This next section is very important because it will show you why sticking with reading more break and dealing with reality will lead to better putting.

Prove it to yourself with feedback

Read a putt your old way, mark your read with a tee, and set up an Aimline at twice or three times the break. Mark the expected ball track with stickers, and replace the ball to be putted. Next place a second ball under the Elevated Aimline one-foot in front of the original ball, and put a third ball on a tee, 1/4-inch to the uphill side of the second ball. This third ball is now your feedback ball (remove the second ball).

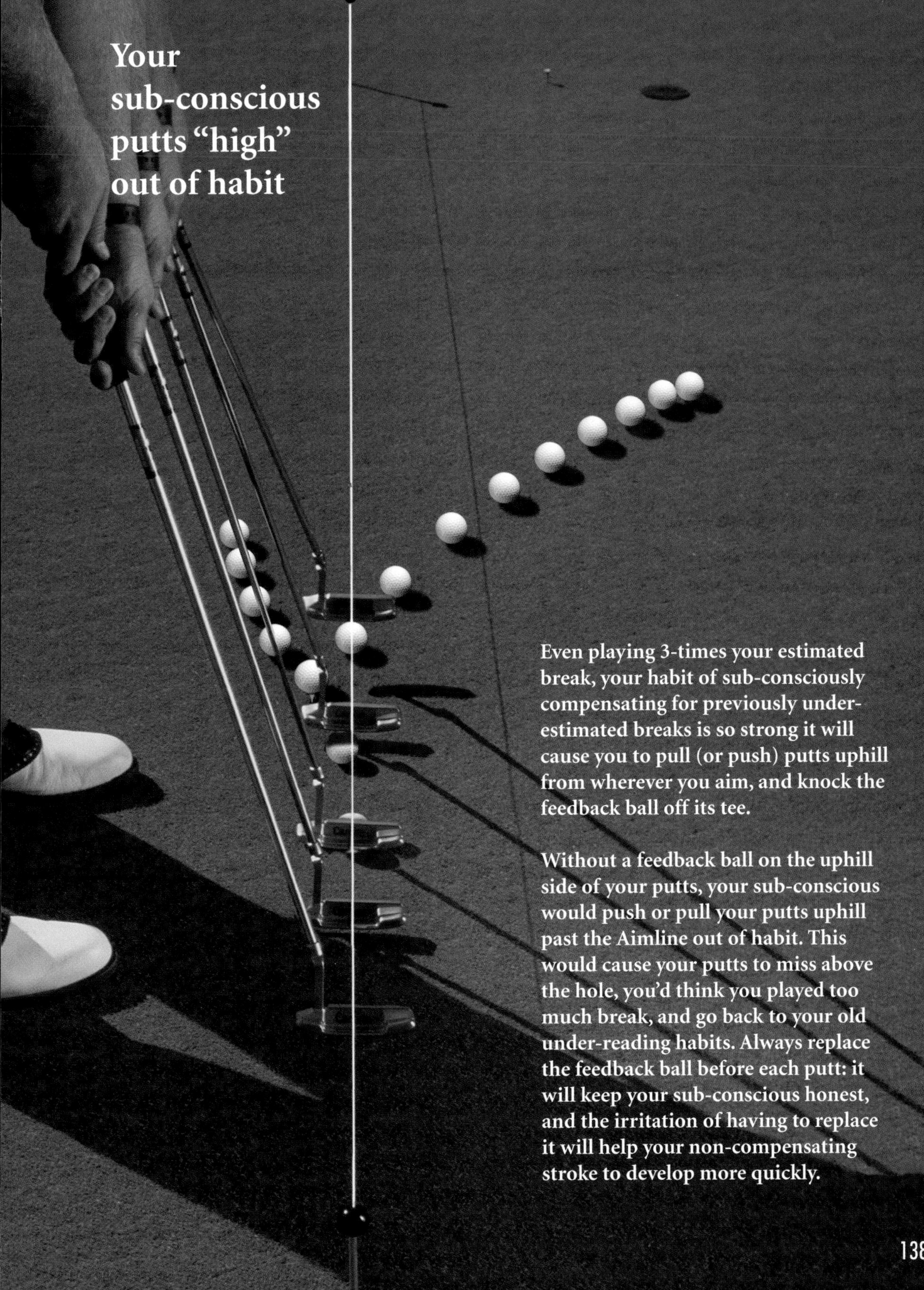

Your sub-conscious putts "high" out of habit

Even playing 3-times your estimated break, your habit of sub-consciously compensating for previously under-estimated breaks is so strong it will cause you to pull (or push) putts uphill from wherever you aim, and knock the feedback ball off its tee.

Without a feedback ball on the uphill side of your putts, your sub-conscious would push or pull your putts uphill past the Aimline out of habit. This would cause your putts to miss above the hole, you'd think you played too much break, and go back to your old under-reading habits. Always replace the feedback ball before each putt: it will keep your sub-conscious honest, and the irritation of having to replace it will help your non-compensating stroke to develop more quickly.

Review why Apex putting misses below the hole

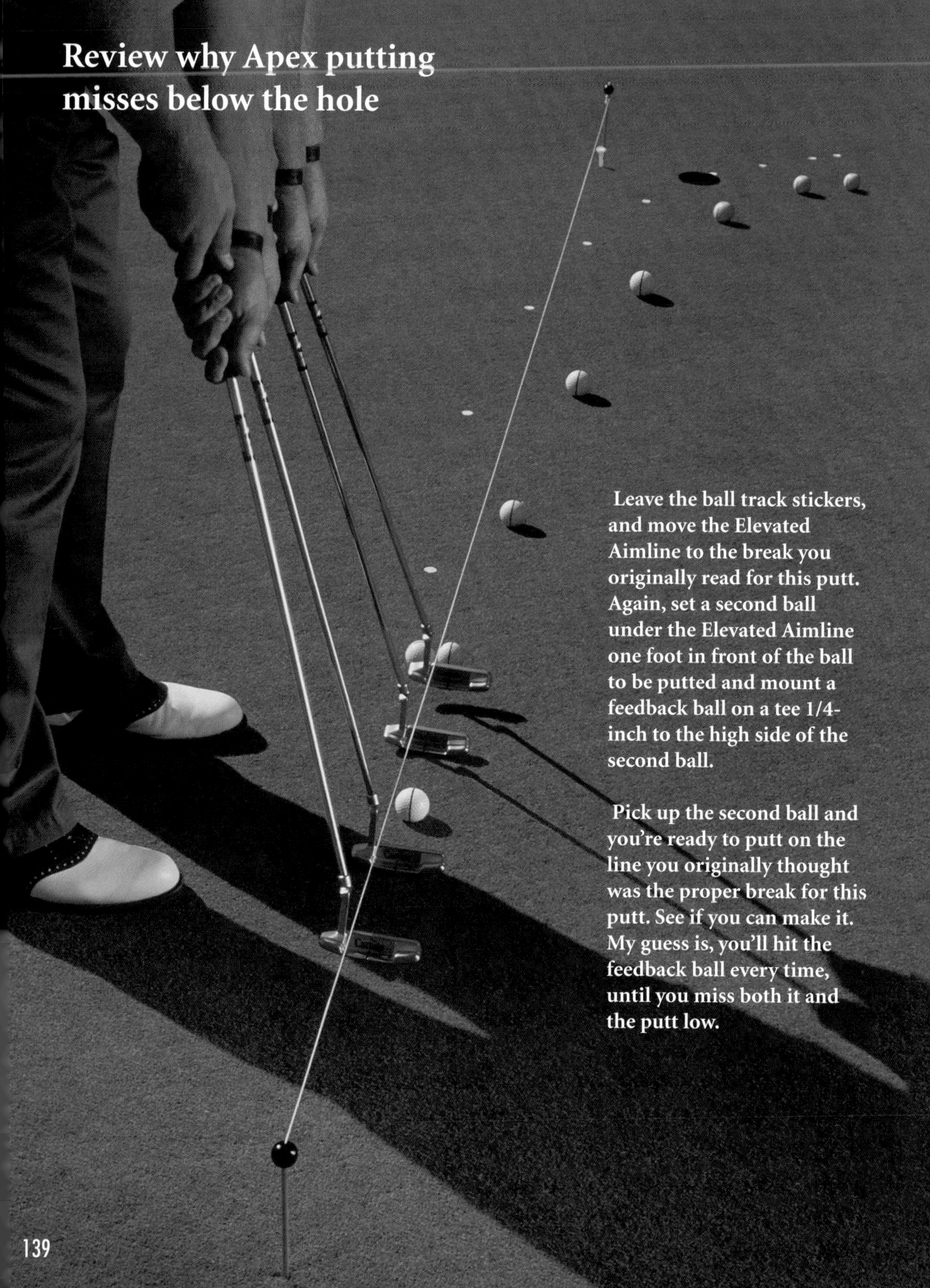

Leave the ball track stickers, and move the Elevated Aimline to the break you originally read for this putt. Again, set a second ball under the Elevated Aimline one foot in front of the ball to be putted and mount a feedback ball on a tee 1/4-inch to the high side of the second ball.

Pick up the second ball and you're ready to putt on the line you originally thought was the proper break for this putt. See if you can make it. My guess is, you'll hit the feedback ball every time, until you miss both it and the putt low.

Train to reality

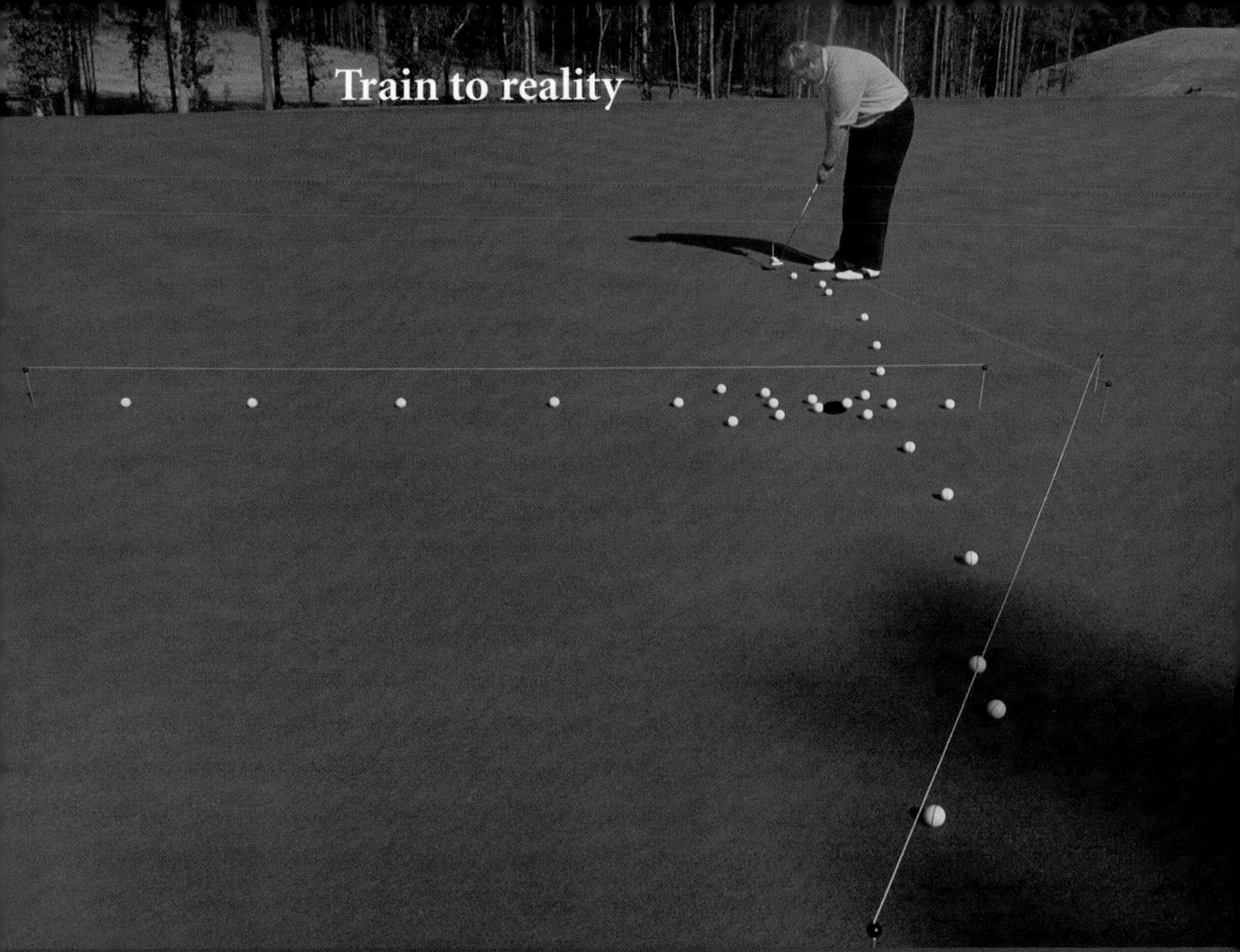

Set up Elevated Aimlines on each of three putts, two breaking in opposite directions, one dead-straight. Add a feedback ball on the high side of each breaking putt Aimline, and adjust the Aimlines until you can miss the feedback ball and make the putt at good speed. Putting around this triangle will train your "mind's-eye" to the reality of the true Aimline and break of putts.

#38 Help your subconscious (open up your mind's eye): Set up perfect Elevated Aimlines and feedback balls for three putts as shown above. Putt each putt twice, then move to the next putt. Not counting set up time (which could take 10 minutes), you can putt all three putts about six times in a 10-Minute Learning Session. This gives you thirty-six chances to re-train your subconscious to make the same non-compensating stroke on straight and breaking putts.

You may need to repeat the session a few times to convince your subconscious to get rid of the compensations it spent years developing.

Re-train Your Stroke

Do you think you could putt better under pressure if you grooved one stroke for all putts? Or would you putt better with a different stroke and a different in-stroke compensation, for every putt?

The answer should be obvious: You want one, repeatable, non-compensating stroke, which always starts putts on the right line so you can concentrate on delivering the optimum speed. This, as much as anything else in this book, is required for putting success. But how can you hope to create this stroke when you can never know for sure the perfect break before you putt?

The answer is a two-step process. First, you must develop the ability to consistently start putts rolling precisely on whatever Aimline you choose. Then you must develop the ability to read the green accurately enough to choose the optimum Aimline (play the proper amount of break) for each putt. Both of these objectives can be accomplished by using a learning aid called the Putting Tutor.

The secret is in making the commitment to start all your putts on the Aimline you choose.

Aim the Putting Tutor and choose the gate spacing you can putt through successfully 50% of the time.

Groove to the Aimline

The Putting Tutor provides feedback that will teach you to orient your stroke precisely to your Aimline. This is important because, due to the sub-conscious compensations I talked about earlier, most golfers do not start their putts in their intended direction. The gate marbles will act as the "high-side-feedback-ball" did on the preceding pages.

Set the Putting Tutor with its Aimline aligned directly at your estimated break point, as shown on this fast, big-breaking putt. From behind your ball, look down the Aimline before each putt. Commit yourself to starting this putt on that Aimline.

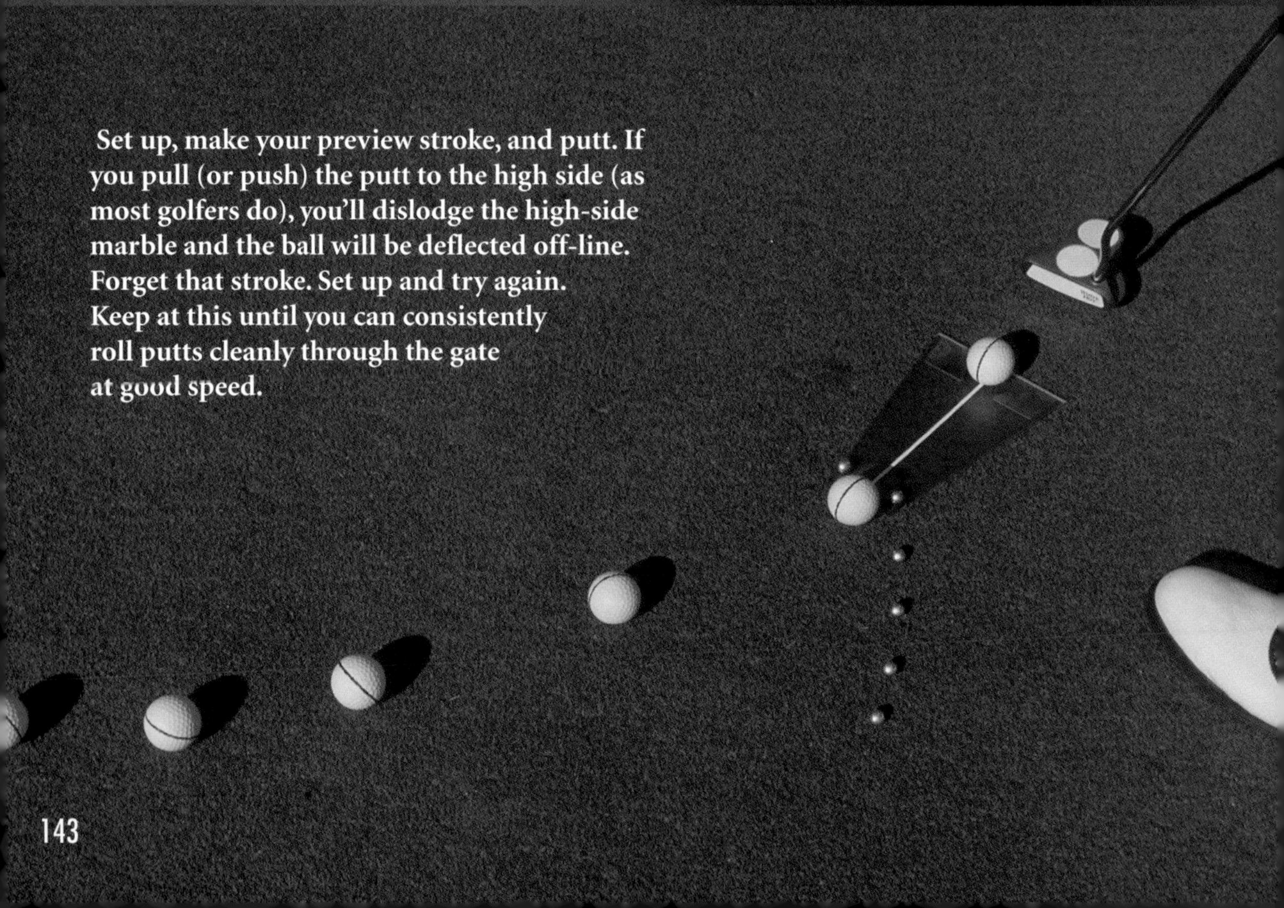

Set up, make your preview stroke, and putt. If you pull (or push) the putt to the high side (as most golfers do), you'll dislodge the high-side marble and the ball will be deflected off-line. Forget that stroke. Set up and try again. Keep at this until you can consistently roll putts cleanly through the gate at good speed.

If your well-struck putts roll cleanly through the gate and misses below the hole, re-align the Tutor by the amount of the miss. You may have to adjust the Tutor's Aimline several times before you get it set to reality, so you can hole the putt at good speed.

After you can start most of your putts through the Tutor gates, set up three Tutors for three breaks as on page 140. You'll find this much easier than setting up the Elevated Aimlines. Putt with two balls from each Tutor, then rotate to the next putt.

#39 Remove in-stroke compensations: Start by using the Putting Tutor on a level putt on a carpet. Aim at a target soda can, block the roll of the balls (so the target doesn't get hit and moved), and roll about thirty putts. To optimize learning efficiency, use the brass marble tolerance gate that you can putt through successfully about 50% of your strokes. When you are up to 80% success, move to using the next tighter tolerance gate.

Don't use the Tutor to work on breaking putts until you can putt consistently on your Aimline on straight putts. Once you learn to set the Tutor up efficiently, you can putt about thirty putts in a 10-Minute Session.

Train to Your Aimline on Known Slopes

The greater the slope of a putting green surface and the lower the surface friction (the faster the green speed), the more severely putts will break on it. If you don't know how to recognize different slopes and different green speeds, you'll never be able to read how much putts will break. This is not a case of intelligence, background, talent, coordination, or strength. It is simply a case of seeing enough slopes and green speeds to recognize them.

I don't have the answer yet for how to learn green speeds in 10-Minute Sessions at home, but I do have it for learning about slopes.

Putt on slopes at home

The Slopemaster Putting System is designed to simulate the slopes you regularly see on golf courses. Precision underlay panels provide three different slopes. If you already have a good putting carpet (and are willing to cut holes in it), you can use your own, or one is available with the system.

Practicing 3- to 9-foot putts on three different (but known) slopes is good for recognizing them. The more you putt on, walk on, and look at these surfaces, the easier it becomes to recognize the same slopes when you see them on the course.

#40 Learn it here, use it on the course: Slopemaster carpets are fun (and beneficial) for indoor practice in the off-season. I have one in each of two home-offices, plus one in my office at work. A good 10-Minute Slopemaster Session will give you feedback on about 40 breaking-putts. You should vary the putt length (between 3, 6 and 9 feet) each session.

Visualization and Green Reading

It seems to me that brains are similar to other muscles in our bodies. They can be stretched, developed, strengthened, and trained. I have seen many golfers learn and improve their ability to read greens. It's happened to me: The more I teach others about green reading and visualization, the better I become at doing it myself.

If you want strong arms, exercise and challenge them by lifting weights. If you want to improve your green reading, exercise and challenge your mind's eye by reading greens, then watch and learn from good feedback as to what actually happens. Create the vision of what you think will happen, then see if it does. The more you visualize with proper feedback, the better your green reading will be in the future.

Exercise Your Imagination

With a Cup Collar, tee, and ball spot, you can start exercising your imagination for green reading.

Drop a Cup Collar on a green 10-feet from your ball, where you're sure a putt would have a sizable break. Walk behind the Cup Collar to see where you think a perfect putt will enter this simulated hole. Orient the Cup Collar entry point (white mark) there. Then walk behind the ball and look to see the entire ball track. Imagine where the Aimline is. Move over and stand on the Aimline (where it extends behind the ball) so you can see where it extends out to the true aim point. Place a tee to mark where you see the true break point to be. Now mark where you think the ball track will hit the apex of its roll. If you really can't imagine where it might roll, put a sticker dot down anyway. You can learn as you go.

Carefully align the
Tutor to your aim
point (tee).

Miss

Make

Verify the Tutor aim from behind the ball. Then address your putt, create your preview stroke, and putt. If your ball rolls cleanly through the gate at good speed, but misses, you read the break wrong.

Adjust your read, move your aim point tee, re-align the Tutor, and repeat the process. The more you hole putts at good speed through Tutor gates while aiming at true break point tees, the better you will learn to read greens.

#41 Stretch your mind's muscle: Set up a Tutor on any putt on your practice green. Read the putt, place a tee at your true break point, and orient a Cup Collar around the hole (entry mark positioned appropriately). Putt using your entire pre-shot routine and ritual process, and repeat the set up (re-aligning the Tutor at new and better break points) until you hole a perfect putt at perfect speed. You should be able to visualize and validate the real break for two putts in a 10-Minute Session.

Rules of Too-High

1) Choose a hole on a slope.
2) Stretch an Elevated Aimline over the hole along the ball hole line.
3) Putt from anywhere on the green. Try to stop your ball as close to the hole as you can, without going into the hole or below the line.
4) Any ball going in the hole or touching the line loses.

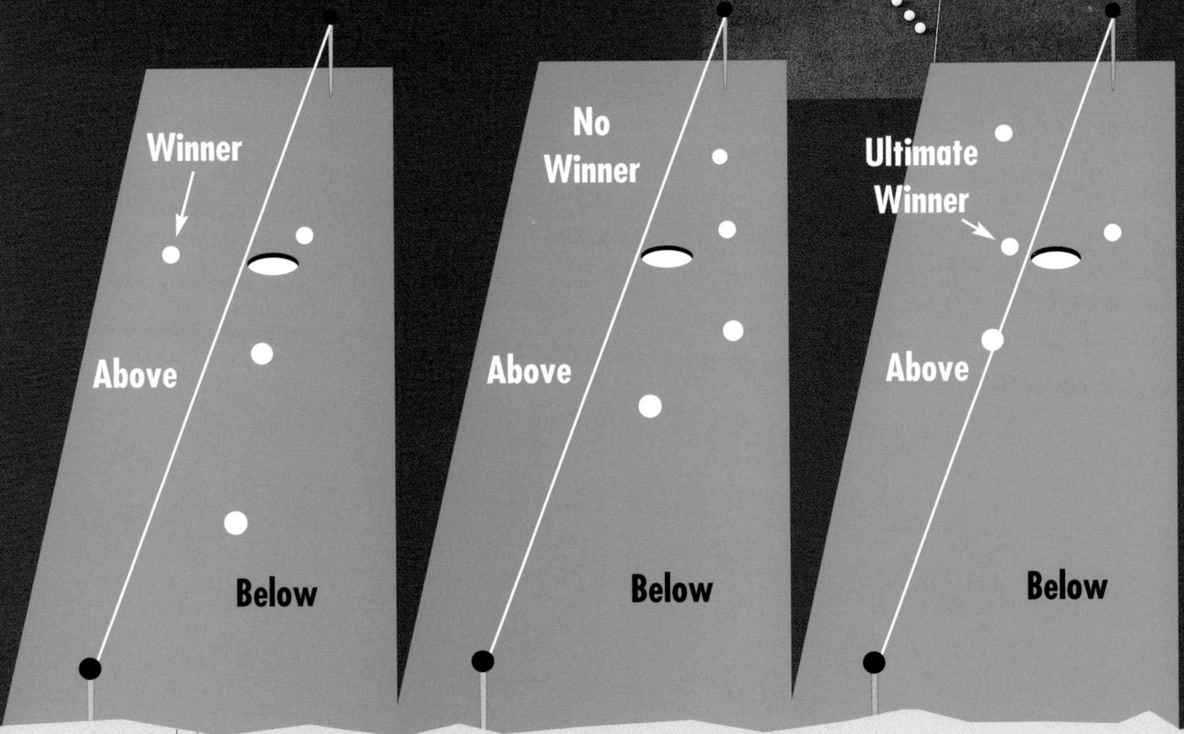

#42 Build your imagination: Set an Elevated Aimline straight along the ball-hole line of any breaking putt. Play 10 minutes of "too-high" in competition and see who can putt closest to the hole without having their ball touch or roll below the line, or go in the hole. If your ball goes in, you lose. In 10 minutes you can play 10 holes of "too-high" with a friend, and in several sessions you'll begin to understand how high too-high is. It's easier to see the optimum line when you know where too-high is.

Hold and Learn

Hold every stroke finish, whether in practice or for the most important putt of your life, until the ball stops rolling or falls into the hole. Let your feel (kinesthetic awareness) combine with your mind's eye vision to learn the correlation between your green reads, your strokes, and your results.

When practicing, putt with O-Balls and use all of the learning aids you can. On the course and in competition, putt with O-Balls to keep an eye on your stroke mechanics, while learning about the greens too.

#43 Learn from feedback: To help keep your ritual and stroke mechanics the same both in play and practice (remember Chapter 3), good alignment and green reading feedback comes from using O-Balls.

It's important to avoid confusion when watching the ball roll. Go to the most sloping putting green you can

Learn from these three putts:

No Wobble
Good Stroke
Perfect Read

No Wobble
Good Stroke
Bad Read

Bad Wobble
Bad Stroke
No Feedback
on Green Read

find, and watch your short breaking putts roll for 10 minutes. Get it clear in your head: you can't learn anything about break from a poorly struck putt, but well-struck putts can tell you all you need to know. Make putt-watching a habit, because there's no better way to learn about green reading than from perfectly rolling O-Balls.

7 Execution

I told you in the introduction this was my "shut-up-and-do-it" book. Well, this is the "shut-up-and-do-it" chapter of that book. Shutting up means stop thinking about improving and start *doing* it.

You will putt better if you've done all the 10-Minute Sessions of this book often enough to execute what they have taught you … out of habit. Then you can putt with the skills you have that day: not thinking about them or trying to make them better. Stay faithful to the way you've prepared yourself to putt, and you'll be fine. Just shut-up and do-it.

Shut Up and Do It

Learning to trust and execute is as important as learning anything else in this book. One of the worst things you can do is stand over a putt trying to make sure you won't do anything wrong. The more you think and worry about what you are going to do, and, in particular, how you are going to do it, the worse things will get. Therein lies the beauty of this book. It is positive and pro-active. It shows you what to do and how to do things for your putting almost entirely in pictures. Leave the rest up to your sub-conscious.

This is not to say I want you to shut down your brain when you putt. Just the opposite. I want you to be alert, creative, sensing, watching, looking, and learning. I want you taking in all the things that can get you in touch with the greens, how your putts will roll, and help you to compete better with the course, other players, and yourself.

You can't think your way through putting

The worst thing you can do over a putt is think about the details. You can't be thinking about your stroke mechanics, your grip, or your stance; it's too late for that. Leave mechanics and technical details to your subconscious, which you've already trained.

The "real deal" is to have your mind actively focused on how your putt is going to interact with the green, on its roll to the hole. Think in pictures. Get a clear picture in your mind's eye of your ball rolling purely, at perfect speed, center-cut into the hole. If this picture is clear as you *feel it* in your routine, then you are free to pull the trigger on your ritual and go.

Fit putting improvement into your lifestyle (improve in comfort)

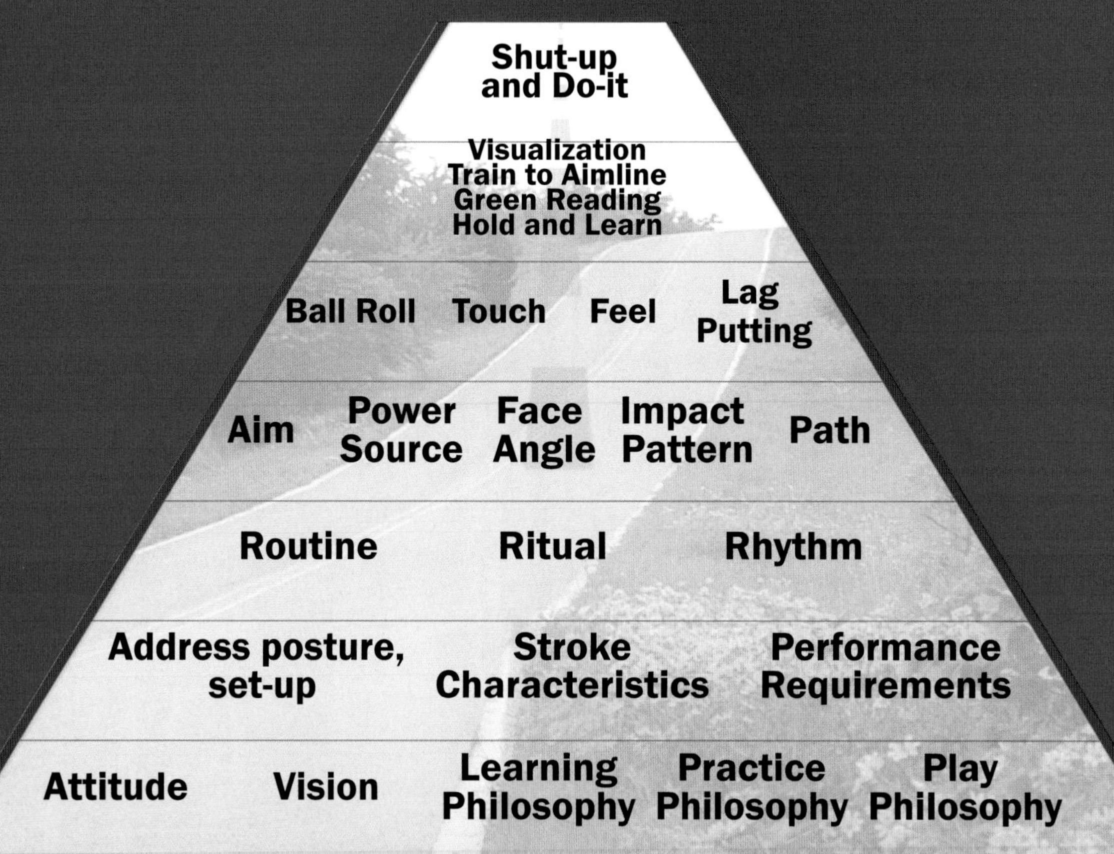

Start at the bottom and go all the way to the top of the putting pyramid, building on what you've learned as you go. Don't think the lessons at the bottom are least important. Read chapters 1, 2 and 3 carefully, because if you don't own that information, nothing else matters. You must build confidence, persistence, and a putting routine and ritual that allow you to change and improve over the years, without everything else falling apart. And, perhaps most important, you must have, or develop, a good attitude.

Be open minded about change, because change is required for improvement (I have this straight from the Pelz dictionary, where you find the definition of Putting Insanity: The act of putting the same way, over and over and over again ... yet continuing to expect better results).

Don't flirt with putting insanity. Once you've decided to do something about your putting, do it right. Working on the wrong things, or working in the wrong way, will do nothing for your putting: No matter how hard you work. Create an area where you can spend 10 minutes at a time without disturbing anything or anybody else. No set-up time, no put-away time. And be comfortable while you do it.

#44 Refine your learning center: In Chapter 1 (page 9) there was a 10-Minute Session on choosing an area where you could efficiently improve your putting. Now it's time to optimize that area, making sure you have all the feedback devices and learning aids you need, and that they are set-up for efficient use. Work on this after you've determined which aspects of your putting need improvement. Make sure you have a television set, good lighting and a good music system, whatever will help you enjoy the time you spend there.

Find Your Weaknesses

There is nothing wrong, or bad, about admitting that you have deficiencies in your putting game. If you didn't, you'd be the best putter in the world and probably playing on one of the pro tours. But you must start by acknowledging that there are parts of your putting that need fixing or improvement.

Identify, then attack, your weaknesses. Every time you identify a weakness, you have found a possibility for creating a new strength in your game. Every time a weakness is turned into a strength, your handicap, your playing ability, get better. If you can turn weak areas of your putting into strengths, you cannot help but be a success.

Nobody's perfect

Do you fear short putts and miss lots of them? If so, you might think fearing or missing short putts is your weakness. Fear however, is not a weakness, it is a result of a problem.

Eliminate the real "problem" (for short putts it could be stroke deceleration, face rotation, a bad grip, a loop in your stroke, or some other fault) and the bad results which cause fear, will go away.

Every 10-Minute Session is designed to provide feedback to help you improve a specific area of weakness in your putting. Once you work on a weakness and fix it, you'll actually look forward to facing it on the course and defeating it. Once you know your putting will be there when you need it, the game becomes much more fun.

How can you locate and identify the weaknesses in your putting game? If you can't come to one of our schools or clinics, where my teaching professionals can analyze and work on your putting, this is a challenge. I suggest you do every 10-Minute Session in this book three times, keeping a list of those that are easy for you (the ones you do well on), and those that are difficult. Then select the difficult ones and attack them. You can't get too good at anything in putting. The courses and the greens are too tough, and getting tougher everyday.

#45 Make a list of your 10-Minute Session results: Of all the 10-Minute Sessions in this book, each is designed to help improve some aspect of putting. Every session should improve your putting in some tiny way (unless you're perfect in that area, and even then it shouldn't hurt you). Put lots of little improvements together and you'll have a big improvement. It's as simple as that: Identify your weaknesses, find out what they are, find out how to improve them, then *do it 10 minutes at a time!*

Now Double-Up

It has been said that only 5% of a human's brain is active during normal activities, which tells me we have plenty of mental capacity to handle new information. It is also true, however, that we can become befuddled when the information we receive is inconsistent, erroneous, or confusing.

What I'm leading up to is that it's a good thing to use two learning aids simultaneously, but only if you don't get confused. Never combine two aids before you are proficient with each one individually. Once you are however, I recommend doubling-up as soon as you can handle the feedback.

Some sessions are easy to combine, others are not. If you don't generate too much feedback with bad performance from one learning aid (clanging noise from a putting track), you may benefit from adding a second. However, if you receive too much feedback, it can be confusing. Don't combine sessions too quickly, before you are ready.

Two lessons are better than one (when feedback is clear and not confusing)

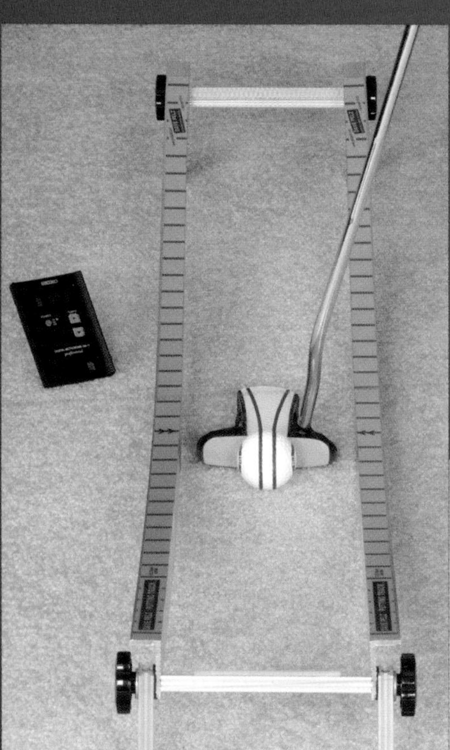

One of your early 10-Minute Sessions should be finding your personal putting rhythm with a metronome. The metronome is one of the first learning aids you can combine comfortably with others.

Whether using a metronome with a Putting Track (for path) or a Truthboard (for face angle), you'll find improved performance when you execute in good rhythm.

The Putting Track and Elk's Key combine feedback on flow line and putter path improvements .

Teacher Clips plus Metronome: Rhythm with solid contact

Shooter plus metronome: Face angle with rhythm

Tutor plus Teacher Clips: Aim, starting line and solid contact

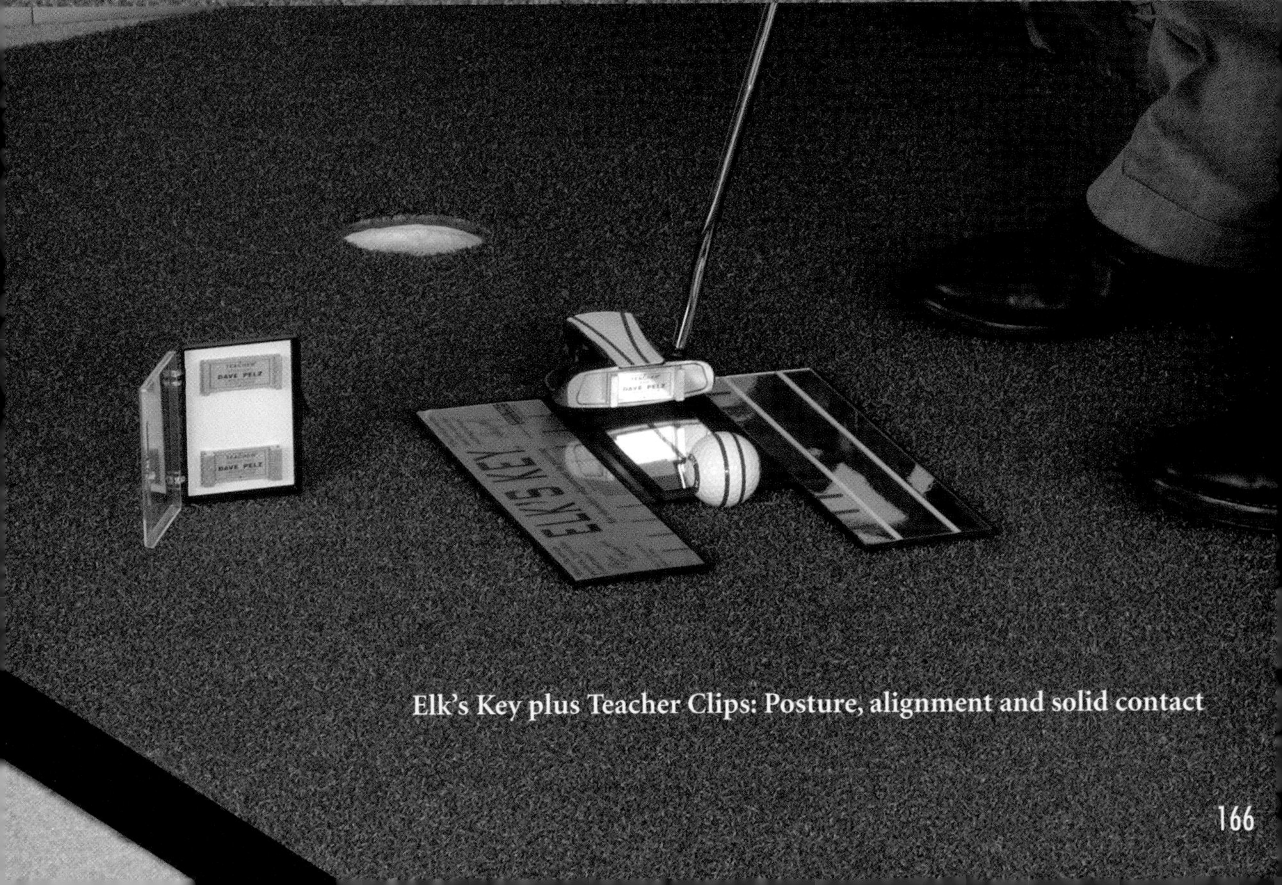

Elk's Key plus Teacher Clips: Posture, alignment and solid contact

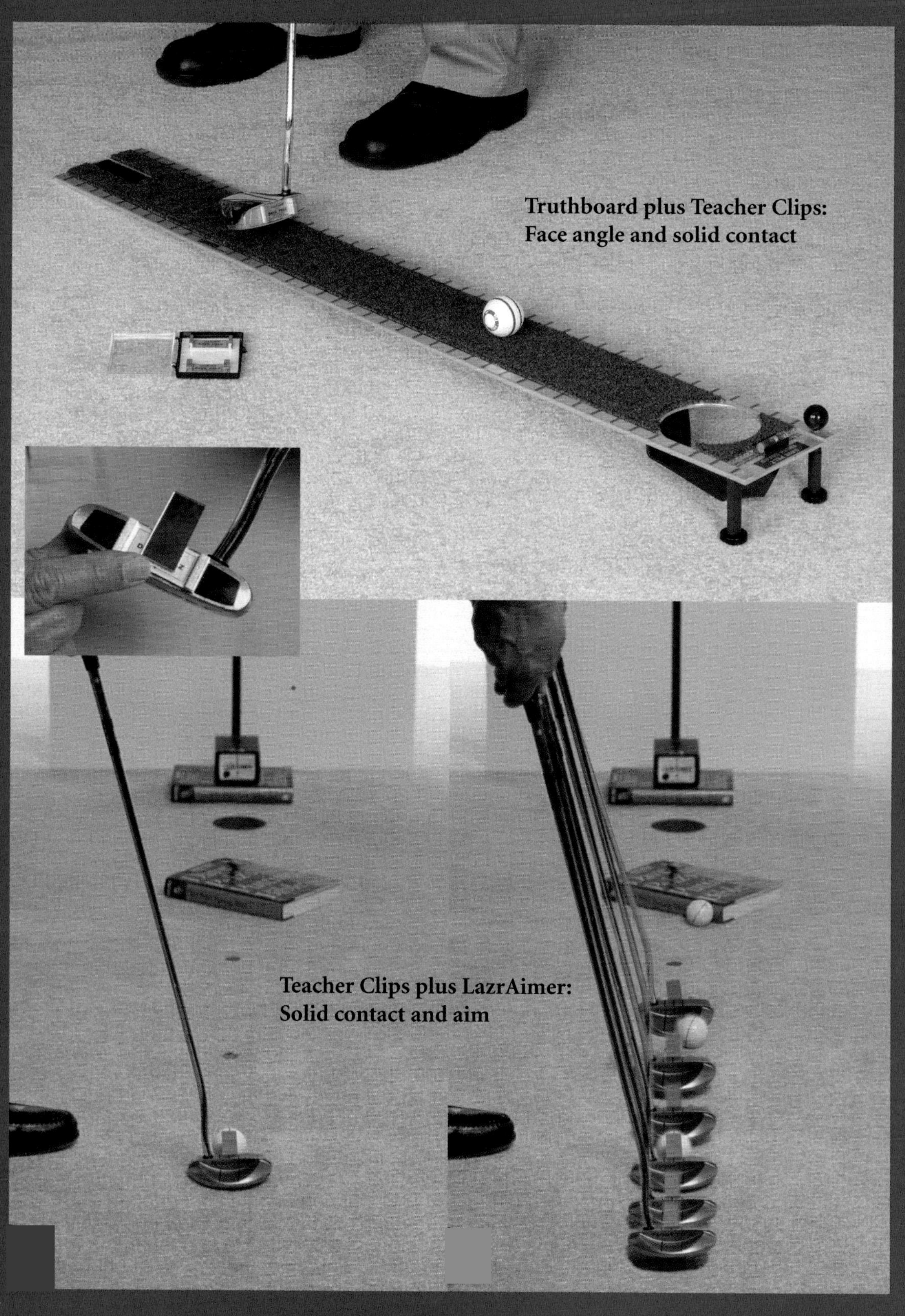

Truthboard plus Teacher Clips:
Face angle and solid contact

Teacher Clips plus LazrAimer:
Solid contact and aim

Putting Track sessions groove your stroke path (straight back and through for conventional putters, curved inside to inside for body and long putters). By adding a metronome, Putting Tutor or Teacher Clips, you receive additional feedback on rhythm, alignment, and quality of impact.

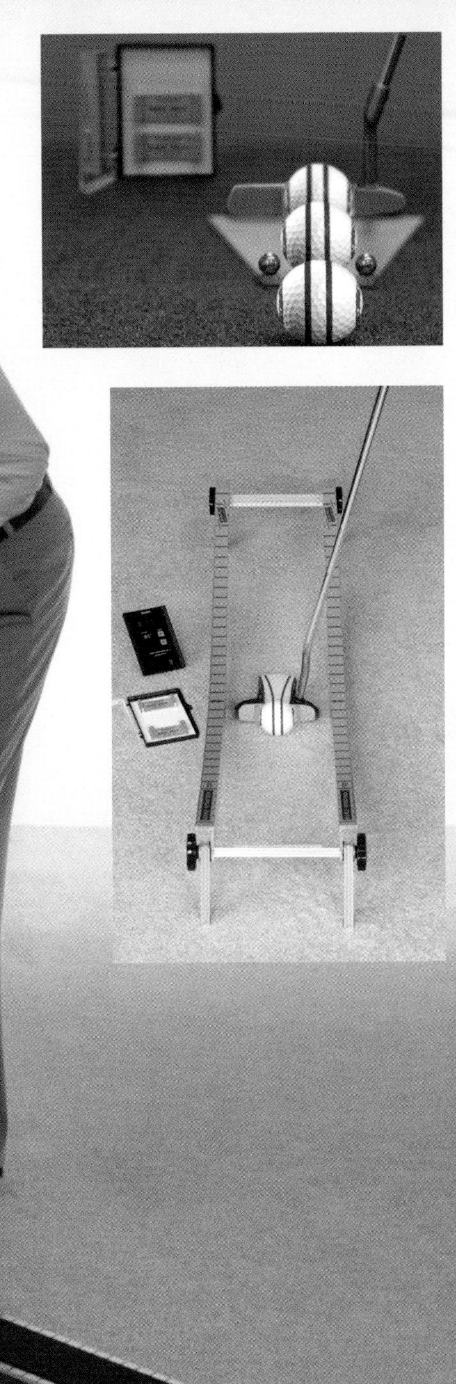

Using the Truthboard in a Putting Track removes fear from short putts. By making quiet strokes and rolling 3-foot putts into a 2-inch hole, your stroke becomes good enough to hole 3-footers on the course, even over footprints.

O-Balls don't count as additional learning aids in these sessions. Their feedback doesn't occur during the stroke; but as you hold your finish, they provide bonus feedback by letting you know how well each putt was struck.

Not all feedback sessions with learning aids are to be conducted indoors. Combine a Putting Tutor with a Phony Hole to optimize your 17-inch-past speed while working on aim and green reading.

Then move to a real hole on a sloped surface and repeat the drill.

#46 Combined Sessions are efficient, and effective: There are many combinations of feedback sessions available to help your putting, and they all have potential for good. But I can't tell you which ones you need the most; that's up to you. You must find out which parts of your putting game are causing you trouble, then improve them. Try other combinations of other learning aids. They will probably work for you too. But I caution you: take the time to learn from each one by itself before you combine them.

Triple-up (or more)

There is no reason to think you can't learn from three, four, or five learning aids at the same time. Just don't think that you'll be learning three, four, or five different strokes. You are always moving toward learning one perfect putting stroke, one way to putt. You are simply getting feedback from multiple sources as you perfect it.

There are multiple aspects of stroke mechanics and mental preparation in putting. This book teaches with feedback from many areas, designed to help you learn one repeatable putting stroke, adjusted only by your feel for the length of each stroke, to fit whatever putting challenges you find.

The more feedback, the better

The more feedback you can handle without confusion, the more efficiently you can learn and improve. Here you can see the Metronome (rhythm), the Putting Track (path), and Teacher Clips (contact), all providing feedback at the same time.

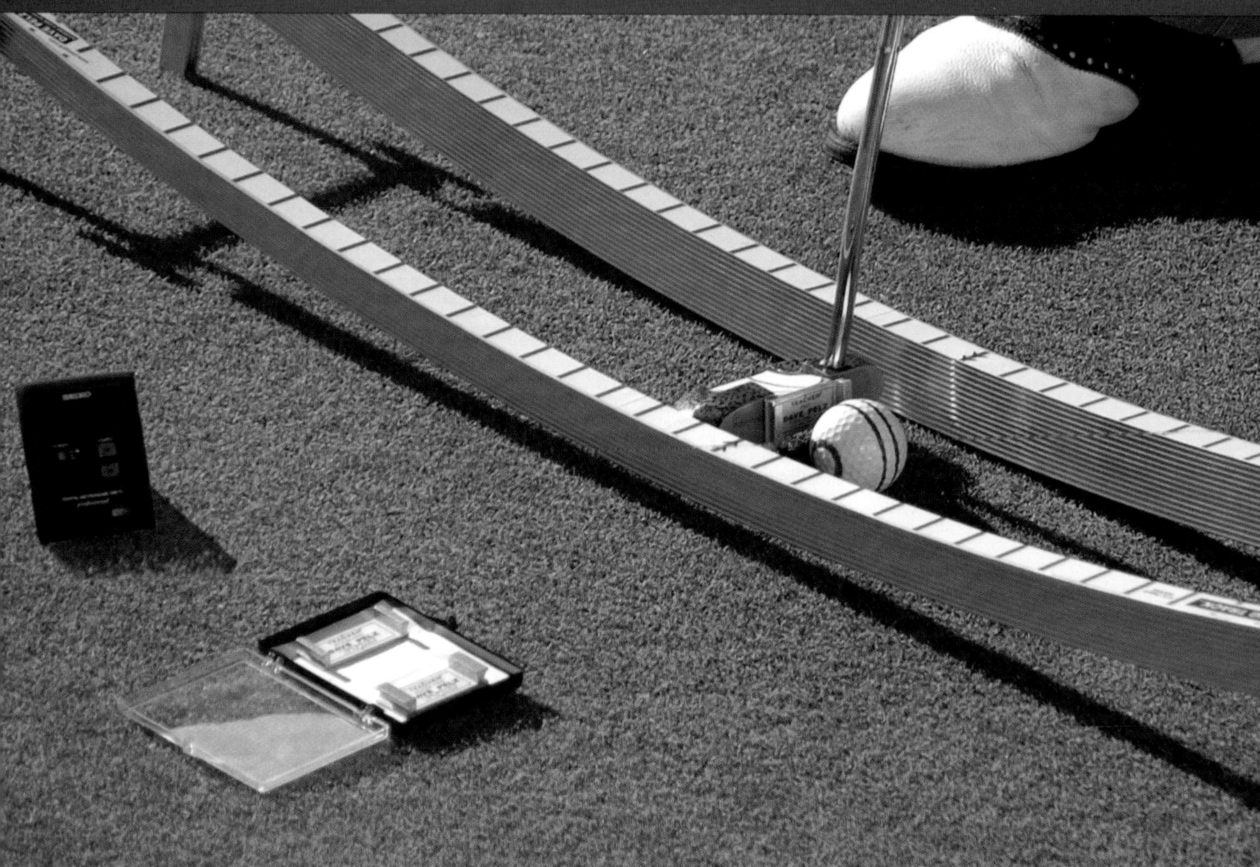

With a Putting Tutor and Track, my aim and path are monitored to perfection, while I also check my speed control with the Phony Hole.

A great breaking putt session is to combine feedback from the Tutor (aim), Teacher Clips (solid contact), and a Metronome (rhythm), on a Slopemaster Putting Carpet.

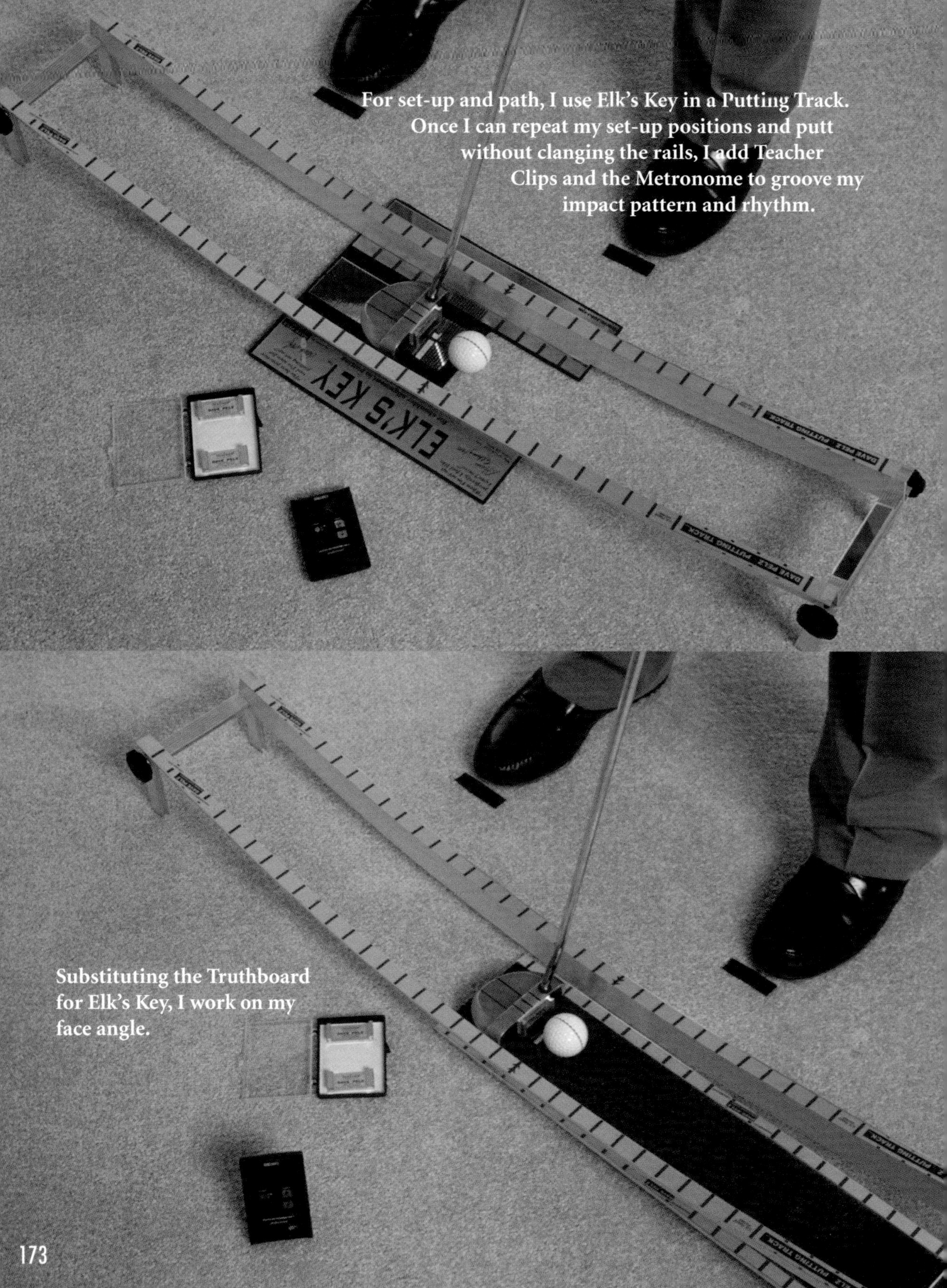

For set-up and path, I use Elk's Key in a Putting Track. Once I can repeat my set-up positions and putt without clanging the rails, I add Teacher Clips and the Metronome to groove my impact pattern and rhythm.

Substituting the Truthboard for Elk's Key, I work on my face angle.

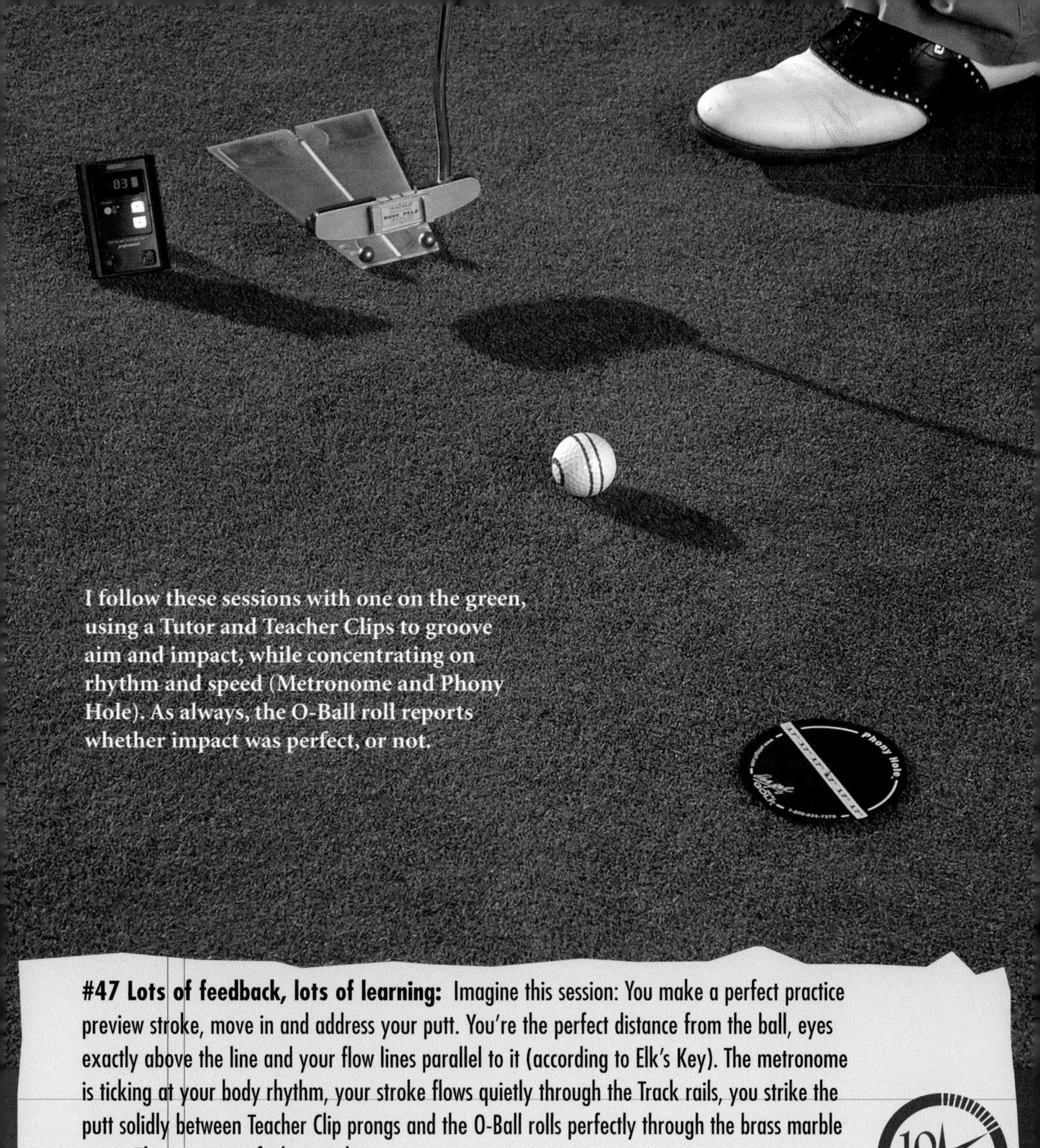

I follow these sessions with one on the green, using a Tutor and Teacher Clips to groove aim and impact, while concentrating on rhythm and speed (Metronome and Phony Hole). As always, the O-Ball roll reports whether impact was perfect, or not.

#47 Lots of feedback, lots of learning: Imagine this session: You make a perfect practice preview stroke, move in and address your putt. You're the perfect distance from the ball, eyes exactly above the line and your flow lines parallel to it (according to Elk's Key). The metronome is ticking at your body rhythm, your stroke flows quietly through the Track rails, you strike the putt solidly between Teacher Clip prongs and the O-Ball rolls perfectly through the brass marble gates. That is a great feeling stroke.

After a few of these strokes, you feel the groove, you relax, you close your eyes, and you make the same stroke again. Perfect! How much better can it get? Not much, except when you do it for 10 minutes at a time often enough that you can take it to the course and hole putts with the same stroke.

Competition is Good Preparation

Spend time working by yourself in 10-Minute Sessions to prepare yourself to be the best you can be. But working alone is not enough. Competition with another player can be the icing on the preparation cake.

When you compete while practicing, it makes you pay attention more, focus more, and try harder on each shot, more like what you do in tournaments. This is great for grooving and getting comfortable with newly learned skills. Competing in games designed to test and provide feedback on your putting skills may just be the best practice of all. Do it whenever you can.

Games (tests) of the World Putting Championship®

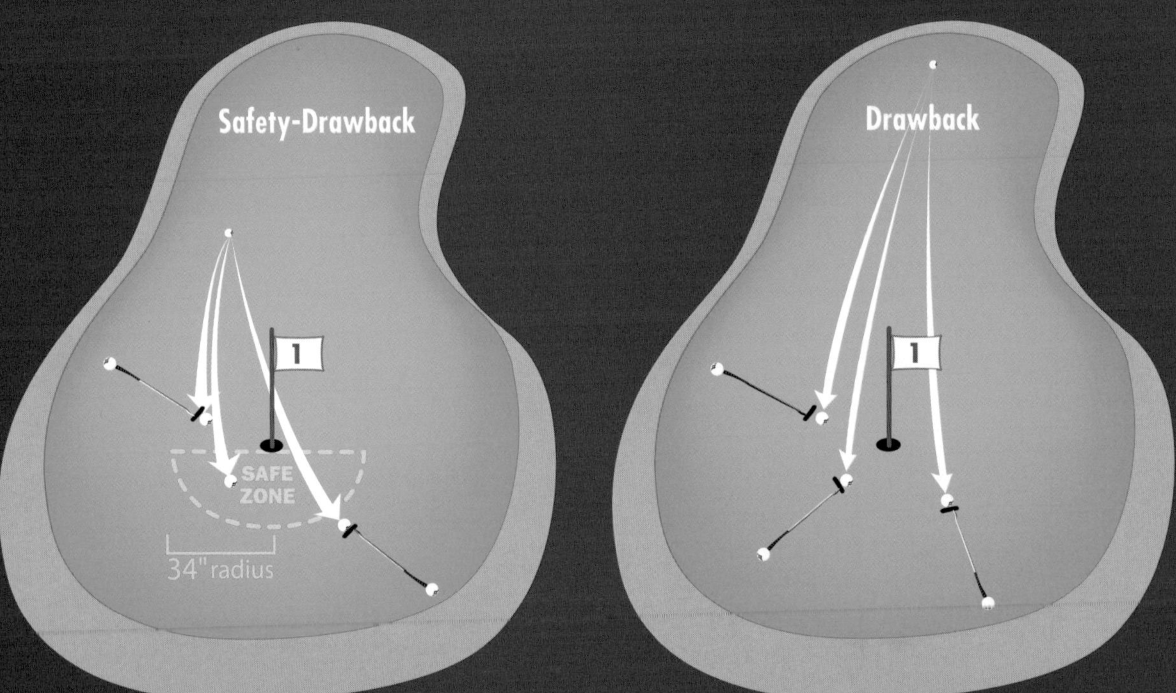

Not all well-struck putts go in, and sometimes poorly-struck putts do. Therefore, luck can play a significant role in determining who putted best if score, or number of putts made, is the only determining factor and the number of putts is not very large.

The WPC concept: Reward well-struck putts (with an advantage) even if they don't go in the hole, and penalize poorly-struck putts with a disadvantage: then determine the best putter as the one who scores best, everything included. This minimizes the influence of luck and lowers the number of putts required to measure putting skill with statistical significance.

Drawback rules are used for lag putts (from outside 35 feet). The skill in lag putting is leaving short remainders and avoiding 3-putts. Good lags come to rest close to the hole, poor lag putts don't. Every putt in Drawback must be drawn back straight away from the hole by 34 inches prior to stroking the following putt. Because putts rapidly become more difficult as they increase in length outside of 3 feet, the 34-inch drawback creates a serious penalty for poor lag putting. Drawback also tests a golfer's ability to hole putts of between 3 and 10 feet.

Safety-Drawback rules are used for make-able putts (from 10 to 30 feet). The ability to hole these putts, and to roll them the optimum speed (stopping in the Safe Zone – the 34-inch half moon behind the hole) is rewarded by being exempt from drawback. Poor speed putts left short, or rolled too far past (not coming to rest in the Safe Zone), are penalized by the one-putter-length (34-inch) drawback. This game also emphasizes the ability to hole 3- to 8-footers.

Double Safety-Drawback rules are used for very make-able putts (inside 20 feet). The ability to hole these putts, or to roll them the optimum speed (into the Safe Zone), is rewarded by being exempt from double drawback – if you putt into the Safe Zone you only draw back one putter length. Poor speed putts left short, or stopping outside the Safe Zone past, are penalized by having to double-drawback (34 inches twice, two putter-lengths). This also tests the ability to hole 9- to 12- foot putts.

#48 Compete with the best putter you can find: The games of Drawback©, Safety-Drawback©, and Double Safety-Drawback© were designed as a series of tests to measure putting skills. Originally used exclusively with PGA and LPGA Tour Professionals, these games were utilized in the World Putting Championships (final 72-hole rounds conducted over eight greens of the Walt Disney World golf complex, in Orlando, Florida).

10 minute

Spending 10 minutes whenever possible playing one of these games (alternate games each session) will optimize your internalization of the skills developed in your indoor sessions. As you compete, analyze which game you do best in and which is your worst. The putt lengths emphasized and tested in each game are different, and can give you good input on what you need to work on in future sessions.

8 Wrap-up

I've spent 28 years studying, conducting research, and learning how to teach putting and the short game (together, the scoring game). My life's work is trying to have the best schools in the world so I can help golfers putt and score better. I hope to spend at least the next 28 years trying to make golfers like you even better, because I love doing it and get my thrills from seeing it work. So please understand that I really mean it when I say there is one thing I've learned for sure … nobody is perfect and we can all putt better.

Make the Play

To optimize your putting, first do all of the 10-Minute Sessions in this book at least three times. This alone will help you to putt better. If you can then determine where you need additional work, you can keep improving by continuing to work 10 minutes at a time, to "nail" your weaknesses.

It doesn't matter where your improvements need to be: in your attitude, set-up, routine, stroke mechanics, or green reading. Do enough sessions so they become boring, so you can let go of the thinking, the control, the mechanics, and the processes of putting, and let your subconscious execute the way you've trained it to. Putt exactly the way you have practiced. If you were smart enough to practice with a good pre-putt routine, ritual, pace, rhythm, and good feedback on your mechanics, then when you putt with the same routine, ritual, and rhythm, you'll putt your best on the course.

It may sound strange, but putting without thinking about mechanics or results forces you to get out of your own way. It may not feel natural, or turn out perfectly the first time you do it, but that's okay. After you've trained properly, let your subconscious putt for you. It's more fun, and not only that; you'll make more putts.

Focus on *vision*. See what you want to do. Get the picture. Read the slope. Visualize the speed. Internalize the conditions. Imagine you're a Tiger. Remember, if you don't know what you want to do, you certainly can't do it.

See It

Focus on *preparation*. Stay in your routine. Create the perfect preview. Feel the perfect stroke. Trust your sub-conscious. Believe you'll make it.

Feel It

Go to tournaments. Watch the great putters. See how they handle the areas you are weak in.

Focus on *doing* it. Execute your ritual. Repeat your preview. Stay out of your own way.
Trust is a must, because to bail is to fail.
Do It
Stand by the practice green. Get as close as you can. Get to know their routines and rituals.

Learn from It

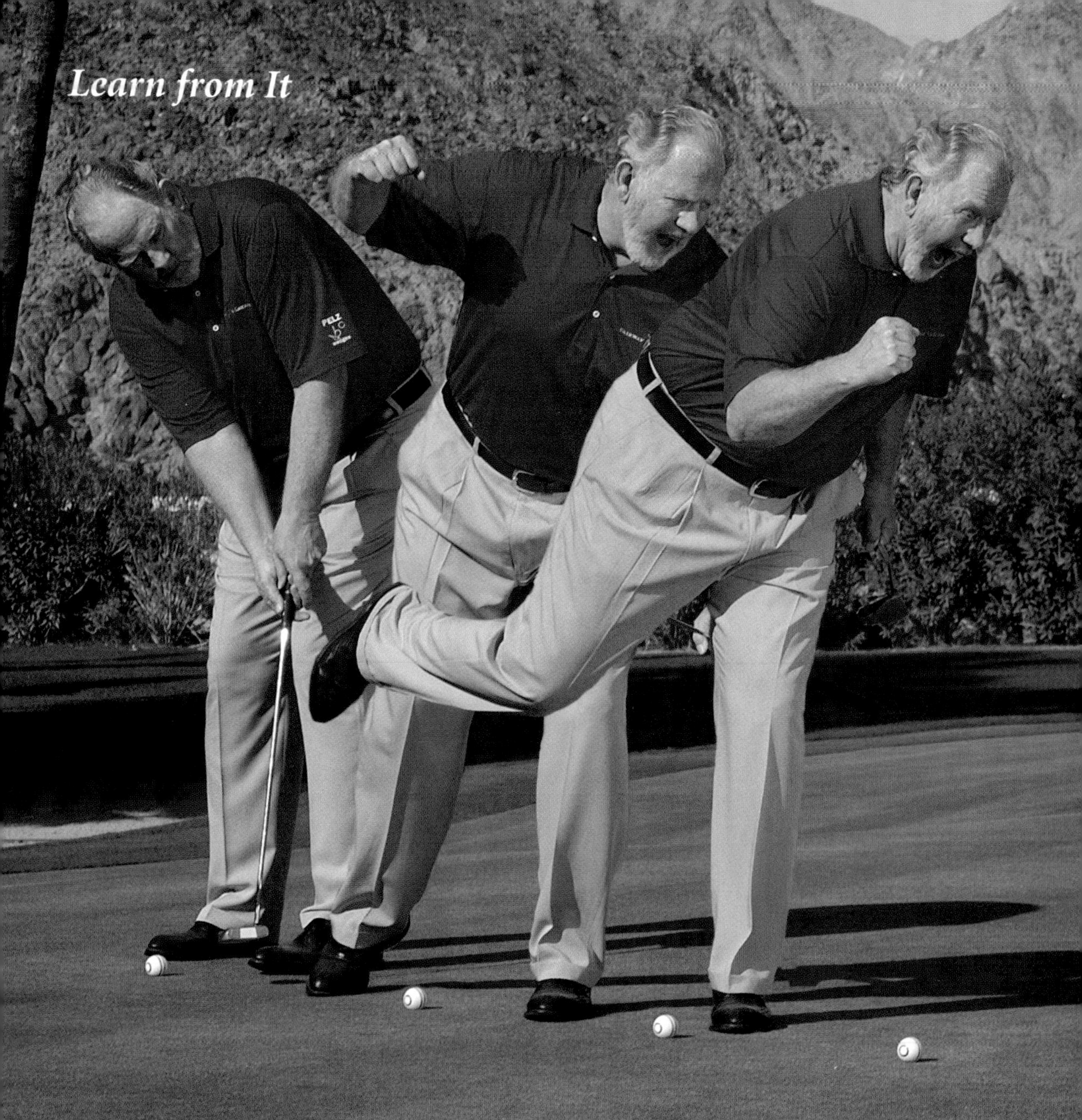

Focus on *learning*. Your ability to focus on the important things in putting is paramount to success. Many golfers learn the fundamentals of stroke mechanics, but never how to perform under pressure, to make a putt when it counts. Pressure can cause anxiety, increased heart rate, fear of failure, fear of success, and an incredible increase in distractions.

Hold your finish until you know the result, then celebrate if you deserve it. The golfer who can focus exclusively on reading the greens and rolling his putts can perform under pressure to his maximum potential.

Learn About Your "Zone"

Learn from your own putting results. Be honest and open in your post-round analysis. If your practice putting is better than your tournament putting, then you are not focusing on what you are supposed to be focusing on. If you are missing more putts below the hole than above, recycle this into a commitment to improve your green-reading and aim. Attack your weaknesses, and turn them into strengths.

Then there is the "zone," the place where players exhibit peak performance. Every player has a different zone and a different bridge to cross to get to it. By zone, I mean the conditions of your mind and body that optimize their interdependence and cooperation, and allow you to perform to your maximum ability. When Tour players get into their perfect stroke rhythm hole after hole, they start seeing the lines and breaks of their putts and they feel, even begin to know, how each putt will roll before it happens. They get into their zone more often than most golfers. So how do you get into yours?

The zone is like a bridge. You have to find it, then learn to let yourself cross it. No one I'm aware of has a formula that works for everyone, but I know that the better you prepare, the better prepared your subconscious will be to help.

You're ready

If you've done your time, done enough 10-Minute Sessions to eliminate your weaknesses and groove your strengths, you are ready. You have prepared your body and mind to perform by subconscious control, by memory, without conscious thought. Now, you must trust yourself.

You have laid the foundation of knowledge, understanding, and determination. They should be able to sustain you through pressure situations and adverse events. You have developed the ability to focus on the job at hand, read the conditions, and roll your ball regardless of outside distractions. Your stroke mechanics are solid, repeatable, and automatic. And if you've done everything properly and seen the good results, you should have confidence that it will all happen if you apply yourself.

It's time to go out, play, and watch the putts drop. Remember, nothing rolls like a ball. All you have to do is get it rolling in the right direction, at the right speed!

Good Putting To You!

KPMG
Consulting
BOSS

Photo Credits

Grateful acknowledgment is made to the following photographers and organizations for permission to reproduce their work:

Leonard Kamsler: Introduction: ii; Ch.1: Pgs. 3; 4B&C; Ch. 2: Pgs. 21 A,B; 22 A,B,C,D,E,F; 25 A,B,C,D,E,F; 28 A; 29; 31; 32 A,B,C,D; 33 A,B,C,D; 34 A,B,C,D; 35; 40 C; 41; Ch. 3: Pgs. 43 & 44; 48 B; 49 A,B,C,D,E,F,G; 52 A,B; 63 A,B; Ch. 4: Pgs. 73 A,B,C,D; 74 B; 76 A,B,C,D,E; 77 A,B,C; 78 A; 80 A,B; 81 B; 84 A,B,C; 85 A,B; 87; 88 A,B,C; 90 A,B,C; 91 A,B; 93 A,B; 97 A,B,C,D,E; 101 A; 102 A,B; 104 A,B,C; 105 A,B; 106; Ch. 5: Pgs. 109; 115 A,B; Ch. 6: Pgs. 127; 128 A,B; 129; 130 A,B; 131; 132; 133 A,B; 134; 135; 137 A,B; 138; 139; 140; 141; 142; 143 A,B; 144 A,B,C; 145; 148; 149 A,B; 150; 151 A,B; 152; Ch. 7: Pgs. 158; 167 B,C,D; 168 C; 173 A,B; Ch. 8: Pgs. 179 & 180; 181. **Fred Vuich:** Ch. 8: Pg. 188 A. **Reynolds Plantation:** Introduction: Front Inside Photo, Back inside photo, Cover; Ch. 5: Pg. 112; Ch. 6: Pgs. 123 & 124. **Boca Raton Resort & Club:** Ch. 5: Pgs. 107 & 108. **Cordillera Lodge & Spa:** Ch. 7: Pgs. 155 & 156. **Golf Magazine by Fred Vuich:** Introduction: VI, C; 0.7.2B; Ch.1: Pgs. 6A,B,C; 12; Ch. 2: Pgs. 27 A,C,D; 42 A,B,C; Ch. 4: Pgs. 83; Ch. 8: Pgs. 183 B; 184 C; 188 B,D. **Centennial Golf/LC Lambrecht '98:** Ch. 2: Pgs. 13 & 14. **PGA TOUR: Copyright 2003 Chris Condon/PGA TOUR:** Ch. 8: Pg. 188 C. **Golf Magazine by Sam Greenwood:** Introduction: VI, B; Ch. 2: Pgs. 27 B; 42 D; Ch. 3: Pgs. 45; 46; Ch. 8: Pgs. 182; 183 C; 184 B. **Andy Lyons/Allsport Inc.:** Introduction: V. **UPI:** Ch. 2: Pg. 26. **Pelz Golf Institute by Joel Mendelman:** Introduction: VI, A; Ch.1: Pgs. 1&2; 4A; 7; 9A,B,C; 10; 11; Ch 2: Pgs. 16 A,B,C; 17 A,B; 19 A,B,C; 20 A,B,C; 23 A,B; 24 A,B; 28 C; 30 A,B,C; 39 A,B,C,D; 40 A,B; Ch. 3: Pgs. 48 A; 50 A,B,C; 51; 54 A,B,C; 55; 56; 57; 58; 59; 60; 61; 62; 66; Ch. 4: Pgs. 70 A,B; 71 A,B,C; 72 A,B; 74 A; 75 C; 79 A,B; 81 A,C,D; 82 A,B,C; 85 C; 86; 89 A,B,C,D; 92 A,B,C; 98; 100 A,B,C,D; 101 B; 105 C,D; Ch. 5: Pgs. 111 A,B; 113; 114; 116 A,B; 118; 119; 120; 121; 122; Ch. 6: Pgs. 147; 153; 154; Ch. 7: Pgs. 160; 161; 163 A,B; 164; 165 A,B; 166 A,B; 167 A; 168 B; 169; 170 A,B,C; 171; 172 A,B; 174; 176; 177; 178; Ch. 8: Pgs. 183 A; 184 A; 185; 186. **Pelz Golf Institute by Adrian Reyes:** Ch. 3: Pg. 65. **Pelz Golf Institute by Sven Nilson:** Ch. 4: Pg. 74C; 78 B. **Pelz Golf Institute by Eddie Pelz:** Ch. 4: Pgs. 67 & 68. **Pelz Golf Institute by Bryan Allison:**Ch. 2: Pgs. 28 B; 16 B; 36 A,B,C,D; 37 A,B,C,D; 38; 40 D; Ch. 4: Pgs. 75 A,B; 103 A,B,C,D,E,F; Ch. 6: Pg. 146; Ch. 7: Pg. 168 A.

The following are registered property of the Pelz Golf Institute:
Aimline®, Dave Pelz Golf®, Elk's Key®, Perfy®, Teacher®, Putting Tutor®

The following have been applied for trademark status by the Pelz Golf Institute:
LazrAimer™, Phony Hole™, Dead Hand's clamp™, Easy Roller™, Slopemaster™, The Shooter™,Pointer™